DON'T KNOW WHERE SHE GETS THAT FROM!

By

Alex Cotton

CHAPTER ONE

Threes a Crowd

So here we were. Now there were three of us. It was our first full day at home as proper, adult, grown up parents, it felt very strange. For all the nine months we'd had to prepare it still felt like it had been suddenly thrust upon us. I wondered if everyone felt like this or if it was my dodgy parenting genes kicking in, after all I had hardly been raised by Mary Poppins. I asked my sister in law Anne if it was normal, she had given birth to her little girl five months before. She said yes, she had felt exactly the same. I didn't know if this really helped when I thought of the delightful parents that she and my husband had, but time would tell. For now, we just knew life was never going to be the same again.

Take going out for example, we couldn't just pop out to the shops anymore. Either one of us had to stay behind to watch the baby or if we both went, we all went. And that was easier said than done. For a tiny little five-and-a-half-pound person there was a mountain of stuff that went with her. We had to take nappies, bottles, wipes, baby bum cream, carry cot, bibs, spare clothes in case of accidents. Her stuff took up far more room in the car than she did.

Not that we would be going out much yet. I was still getting over the caesarean and hobbling around like as old lady but at least I was back in my normal clothes. Because I had only put on around half a stone, as soon as she popped out I was back to my normal size. For some reason this had annoyed the bitchy midwife that had been sent to check on us no end.

Back then you were sent a midwife to check on you and your baby for the first week. As usual, when it came to us there had been a slip up and we were sent two. The first one (Bitchy) was about forty. As soon as she arrived she looked me up and down and asked how old I was.

"Nineteen and a half." I told her (the half was important back then).

"Good God, that's horrific." She said.

"Is it, why?" I asked.

"I've got a daughter that age, Jesus, I could be a grandmother."

I thought that was a little uncalled for but said nothing. Then she wanted to look at my war wound to make sure it was healing properly. She had a look and then asked me how much weight I had put on during the pregnancy. When I told her half a stone she sneered.

"Well you might be back to your normal weight but you'll never have a flat stomach again." What a peach this one was.

After she had finished insulting me she turned her attention to my daughter. As it was a hot day I had dressed her in just a cotton baby grow and she was sleeping, quite happily in her carrycot in the coolest part of room. Nurse Bitchy took one look and told me to get those clothes off that baby at once, was I trying to give her a heat stroke? I told her she didn't feel as if she was too warm but she had already woken her up by dragging her clothes off.

She left her in just her nappy and told me to leave her like that until the sun went in later. I thought she was over reacting, it's not as if I had her stretched out on a sun lounger, soaking up the rays but what did I know. She went through a few more things with me, rolling her eyes at most of my answers. I began to think this woman had been trained by Dr Patronising from the hospital. Her last question was,

"Have you moved your bowels?"

I felt like saying "Have you?" By this point I was sick and tired of being asked that question. From the moment I had woken up from the operation it seemed like every other person wanted to know about my toilet habits. It was a bit too personal for my liking. For the last nine months I had been probed, prodded, poked and peered at, I thought that now it was over I would be able to regain some of my dignity but they were still at it. I told her everything was fine in that department thankyou and she got her things together and said she would be back tomorrow. Ooh, I would look forward to that.

About an hour later there was a knock on the door and midwife number two was on the doorstep. This one looked about seventy, she can't have really been that old or she would be retired but she certainly looked that age. I told her the midwife had just left but she insisted on coming in, she had her orders and I was on her list.

She came in, took one look in the carry cot and went mental. What on earth did I think I was doing, leaving that baby half naked, was I trying to kill her from hyperthermia? Oh no, here we go again. I told her the other midwife had just taken all her clothes off (the baby's, not her own). She said all new babies needed clothes on at all times because they had no fat on their bodies to keep them warm.

I put the baby grow back on again but she said that wasn't enough, she added a cardigan, mittens and a woolly hat. Now I might not have been an expert yet but even I knew this was too much, indoors in the middle of a heatwave.

When she had finished suffocating my new daughter she started on me. Once more I told her I had been through all this an hour before but she insisted on doing it all again. She checked my scar, asked me all the same things and finished up with the usual,

"Have you moved your bowels?"

By now I was finding it hard to resist, I really, really wanted to say,

"You know what, I did, I moved them this morning and I can't remember what the hell I did with them."

I could tell by her face that she wouldn't find this amusing though so I bit my lip and told her yes, my bowels were working just fine and dandy thank you.

Before she left she said she would be back tomorrow. I told her we already had a midwife, there must have been a mix up but she said I was on her books so she would be coming every day for the next week. Great.

As soon as she had gone I took all the winter woollies off my daughter, who was already starting to turn purple. I left her in her vest and nappy with the rubber frilly pants over the nappy, no disposables back then. Well actually they were just coming in but they were like giant sanitary towels held in place by a plastic bag like contraption, I had bought some and tried them out while we were still in hospital. It wasn't a great success, the poor little mite had an immediate reaction to the plastic and came out in big red splodges so we binned them and went back to nappies and rubber pants.

Apart from the red and blotchy look she had also tried the jaundiced look while we were still in the hospital. A lot of the babies had this at the same time, after the first day or two they all turned yellow. Not Simpsons yellow but still yellow. The hospital's solution to this was to put them under ultra violet lights for a few hours a day. They covered their eyes with little pads first to protect them. I used to go and watch my daughter under the lights. Stretched out, eyes covered, a fetching shade of yellow, she looked like the world's smallest orange celebrity by today's standards.

Throughout that first day we were besieged by visitors, all wanting a look at the new arrival. Various friends, relatives and neighbours all stopped by with gifts for her, I began to worry where I would put them all, after all we were still in our one bedroomed flat at this point. It was becoming more apparent by the minute that we would be needing a bigger place, especially being three floors up. If the lift was out of order on the days I was by myself I had no idea how I would get a baby, pram and shopping up the stairs. It would take some organising.

After everyone had seen the baby and had a cuddle they all wanted to see my scar. Apparently, I was the first person everyone had ever known to have a caesarean birth and they were all interested in seeing the exit route. I had escaped being cut from top to bottom as recently it had become the 'done thing' to cut side to side quite low down. It was called the 'bikini' cut, which made it sound quite fashionable. I had a friend who had been cut the other way a few years before me and she had a scar that left her stomach resembling a Cornish pasty.

One by one they peered at my stomach, most of them coming to the conclusion it was very neatly done and the surgeon must have been good at needlework. My new Nanna said the doctor must have had a very steady hand while my mother said the bit on the end looked like my brother's cross stitch tapestry that was hanging on their wall at home. My dad just left the room in a hurry anytime anyone mentioned wanting a look. Eventually, everyone left us to it and we tried to relax and get used to this parenthood lark. We set about trying to bath the new arrival without drowning her and I thought we did quite a good job, she didn't cry much and as she didn't have much hair we didn't get shampoo in her eyes. All in all, as first baths go I thought it was quite successful.

A few hours later, after she had been changed, fed and burped again she was once more back in the carry cot having another forty winks. I put some washing on and sat down to watch a bit of telly. My husband went to put the kettle on and, as he passed the cot let out a shriek of panic. I almost died of fright, now what?

By the time I covered the few steps to the cot he was already ripping off the rubber pants that covered her nappy.

"Look at her legs" he shouted, "they're blue!"

Indeed they were, what neither of us had noticed was the legs of the pants were too tight and were cutting off her circulation, sending her little legs a scary shade of blue. We took a leg each and massaged them until they were pink again, while she slept through the whole drama. Then we had to sit down to get over the shock.

It was ironic really. All that time in hospital I had been convinced I had given birth to a one-legged baby and now that she was home I had very nearly taken both legs away from her. It was a scary thought and after that we watched her legs in shifts until I could get to the shops the next day for bigger rubber pants with looser elastic. We both agreed it was probably best if we kept this little mishap from Bitchy and Oldy when they came back tomorrow, the last thing we wanted was for them to set Social Services onto us before we'd even started this properly.

I felt guilty about it for ages but looking back it was probably the same sort of thing that happens to everyone. What new parent doesn't tell the tale of the day they almost caused their new-born's legs to drop off?

CHAPTER TWO

Happy Travellers

Over the next few days we tried to get out and about a bit. It was far too hot to stay in the flat so we packed up what felt like half of Mothercare and went off on our travels. For the first week, we had to hang around every morning until Nurse Bitchy and Nurse Oldy had done their daily visits. Whatever had happened with the mix up it was still going on and neither of them would back down and let the other one take over. It didn't help that they both had completely opposite ideas on how babies should be looked after. In the end, it was easier just to go along with whichever one was there at the time.

We would watch out of the window every morning to see which one would arrive first then, while they were making their way up to the flat I would either undress my daughter down to the bare essentials or add several layers of winter woollies according to which one turned up.

We did a bit of visiting to the grandparent's houses and a couple of times on our little excursions we went off to the seaside,

Bridlington or Scarborough. The last few times we had been to these places there had only been two of us and we were on a motorbike. Things were very different now we were pushing a buggy around. Everything had to be planned around feeding times so we spent a lot of time sitting in cafes or on benches on the seafront, trying to eat fish and chips with one hand while changing a nappy with the other. It put me off curry sauce for a good few months. Wherever we went we couldn't go more than a few steps without some old lady stopping us to look at the baby, they all wanted to know the same things. How old was she, what had we called her, how much did she weigh, was she good? It was quite sweet at first but after about the first twenty times I felt like hanging a sign around her neck with all the relevant details on it.

Over the years both before and after baby we spent lots of times at Bridlington and Scarborough, sometimes Withernsea, we went so often we could find our way there blindfold. Anywhere else we attempted to go we could never manage without getting lost. Huge chunks of our lives have been lost, stuck in villages in the back of beyond, travelling on motorways heading in the opposite direction to where we were supposed to be going and heading 'North' every time we saw a road sign, even though in actual fact we live in the East.

Once, not long after the wedding we went to Doncaster for some reason I can't remember now. On the motorway coming back we started arguing over whether the car behind us was a Ford Cortina or a Ford Granada. We were so busy bickering that we completely missed our exit so kept going, heading North. Every time we came to another sign that said North we followed it. We began to suspect things weren't right after about three hours, the journey to Doncaster had only taken around an hour. We carried on a bit further until we came to the motorway service station and decided to pull in and have a rethink. I think we finally twigged things had gone a bit wrong when we realised most people were talking in a Newcastle accent.

It took us another four hours to get back home and as we were running out of petrol we had to spend half of the next week's rent money to get back. We carried on bickering most of the way home, blaming each other for not paying attention to the road signs. I think we would have been better off paying more attention in geography at school so that we actually knew whereabouts in the country we lived. Eventually we made it back just before bedtime, tired, hungry and bad tempered. After a quick bite to eat we went to bed to try and grab some sleep before we had to get up for work. I was still mad though and I had to have the last word. I lay awake until I heard my husband start to fall asleep, then I leaned over and whispered lovingly in his ear.

"It was a Cortina!"

Things have never really improved since then. Whenever we have to travel anywhere we set off with the best of intentions armed with maps and clear directions but it never works out. We always end up stuck in laybys, maps upside down, arguing over which line is a B road and which is a canal. For the first few years I was always the navigator and had a pretty good idea (I thought) of where I was going but my other half never trusted me and would go off in another direction, getting us hopelessly lost.

Even today, now that we have sat-nav he is no better. He doesn't trust the woman on the sat-nav, he thinks she's trying to trick him and he actually argues with her, it's incredible. She will say,

"At the next junction turn left."

"No" he says, and carries straight on. The poor woman tries again,

"At the next roundabout take the first exit, left."

"No."

"Carry on for half a mile then at the crossroads take a left."

"Shut up you silly cow, I know where I'm going."

It's unbelievable, she'll be telling him left, I'll be shouting left but he flatly refuses to go left because 'it doesn't feel right' (no pun intended). Without fail we always end up doing U turns, heading in completely the wrong direction while the poor woman has a nervous breakdown and starts screaming,

"Recalculating, Recalculating", like a demented dalek.

He has a theory though, every time we get lost (yet again) he tells me it's because that stupid woman's got P.M.S.

He wouldn't be any better if it was a man's voice on the sat-nav though, he just always thinks he knows a better way.

Even travelling with a stubborn person who completely ignores directions and gets us lost nine times out of ten beats the travelling I did with my parents though. Over the years, I tried to come up with more and more original excuses to avoid travelling anywhere with them but sometimes it just couldn't be avoided.

When I was younger and my brother was little I was dragged on endless coach trips with them. If there's one thing they really enjoyed it was a good coach trip, the further away the better. My mother especially loved the ones where some bright spark wanted to start a sing song, she would be in her element then. Showing the rest of the bus how ten green bottles should really be sung, very loudly, as if you were in an opera.

My dad would always opt to sit with my little brother, preferably a few seats away so he could pretend he didn't know the madwoman shrieking away while the rest of the bus were wincing. For some reason, back then my brother was always wearing a bus driver's hat. My dad had bought him some model buses and convinced him he should be a bus driver when he grew up, I've no idea where this mad notion had come from. At some point during the trip my dad would always get the bus driver to let my brother sit in the driver's seat and so there are lots of photos from those days of my brother sitting behind massive steering wheels, wearing his bus driver's hat and a bemused expression.

Meanwhile I would be stuck sitting next to my mother, trying to read my latest comic and praying to be suddenly struck deaf. Now and again she would dig me in the ribs and tell me to stop being a misery and join in, but I never did. If only the Walkman had been invented sooner I would have far fonder memories of my childhood. By the time the green bottles were down to two I would be ready to beat her and myself to death with a rolled-up Bunty, Jackie, or whatever the magazine of that decade happened to be.

It never stopped when the last green bottle had fallen off the wall either. She would immediately launch into 'One man went to mow', dragging the rest of the bus along with her.

One of her other little habits was to announce the name of every town or village we passed through, very loudly and very drawn out. For example, Hunmanby would become **"HUNMANBEEE."** I think in a past life she must have been a tour guide. There was a small village we often passed through called Thorngumbald, this one amused her no end. She would announce, very loudly **"THOORRRNINGUMBALD!"** completely mispronouncing it. She was completely oblivious to the looks from the other passengers (and me and my dad). She still does it to this day, street names, shop names, you name it she will announce it, even when there are only the two of us in the car. I can be halfway through negotiating a particularly difficult roundabout when she will suddenly let loose with **"NORMINGTONNNN AVENUUUUE"**, screamed into my left ear. It can be quite disconcerting.

I just thank my lucky stars we never got as far as Wales on our travels, if we had ever entered the village of Llanfairpwllgwyngyll I think her head might have actually blown off.

CHAPTER THREE

On My Own

The next few weeks went by really quickly. We soon got the hang of this parenting lark and it started to feel perfectly normal. My husband went back to work and we were left to manage on our own. My mother and Sheila were always there if I needed them though with handy little tips on bringing up babies. Needless-to-say I avoided these at all costs, I had seen their parenting skills close up. My mother's consisted of regular slaps to the backside while screaming blue murder, while Sheila's particular area of expertise was to throw a slice of bread and jam at your child as you threw them out onto the street and locked the door behind them. I had never seen any of these handy little tips in any of the baby books.

I must admit though that both of them were better Grandmothers than they had been mothers. My mother was especially proud of being a Grandma (it had to be Grandma, never Nanna), and went around bragging to everyone about her beautiful granddaughter. She was especially determined to be the favourite Grandma as well and shove Sheila out of the picture. Sheila was also trying the same thing but her heart wasn't really in it. She had two baby granddaughters now and the novelty was wearing off a bit. In front of other people, she would play the doting Nanna but whenever we visited it was obvious she was watching the clock, waiting for us to leave. I had a hunch she wasn't going to be the number one babysitter.

I was a bit nervous about leaving my daughter with my mother though after my early childhood experiences. She was no longer a mad knitter as she had been then so that wasn't my main fear. I knew I wasn't going to be faced with a baby dressed in multi coloured trouser suits and hats with big pointed ears on them on my return. I had worse things to worry about than that. I had vowed that as soon as my daughter could understand what I was on about I would drum it into her that if she ever saw her Grandma coming towards her with a pair of scissors in her hand she was to run screaming as fast as she could in the opposite direction. If Grandad wasn't about, run next door and ask Aunty Joan for help. I was going to show her some photos of my early haircuts so that she could better grasp how serious I was about this.

My mother never really got over her urge to give us a quick trim, that's why, in all of my brother's childhood photos he looks as if his head has been in a nasty accident with a lawnmower. Maybe that's why my dad made him wear the bus driver's hat every time they went out in public.

Even today, whenever I visit my mother she spends half the visit trying to push my hair 'out of my eyes' and I know from experience not to let my attention wander for a minute. All it takes is one moment of lapsed concentration, getting too engrossed in what shade of orange David Dickinson is on the telly today and she'd be hacking bits of hair off with the kitchen scissors.

Anyway, while my mother was busy bragging to everyone about her new granddaughter, my dad was busy taking endless photographs. He was always very big on photos, not just for special occasions but for everyday events as well. Every time we walked through their front door a flash bulb would go off in our faces, I started to think I would have to invest in a pair of baby sunglasses to protect my daughter's eyes from all the unexpected flashes. Most of the photos my parents possessed of me back then were of me looking startled, as if I had just had a bad shock. I had, I was constantly being ambushed by a mad photographer. He missed his calling working in a factory, he should have been a member of the Paparazzi.

My dad took photos of everything my daughter did. There are pictures of her sleeping, drinking, eating, crawling, vomiting, even one where she is posing next to the big wet patch when she had a little 'accident'. He could never wait to get them developed and would always use up the last of the roll of film on any old rubbish, just so he could get down to the chemist and get it developed. That meant after you had looked at twenty odd baby pictures you would suddenly find yourself looking at the gas fire, the cooker, a pair of slippers, any old thing that he had snapped away at, impatient to get to the end of the roll. The man at the chemist must have thought he was mad.

It wasn't always baby pictures though. One year, he was so proud of how his garden had turned out that he went around snapping pictures of every flower, plant and vegetable out there. When the pictures came back we all sat there oohing and aahing at all the pretty flowers when all we had to do was walk ten steps outside and look at them for real.

As mad as he drove us with his picture taking, at least all his photos (except the last few in every batch) had people in them. My brother was completely the opposite. When he grew up he took lots of trips abroad and saw all the major tourist attractions, he went all over the world, snapping photos and filled endless albums with lovely pictures. The only trouble is there is absolutely no proof that he was ever there, he doesn't appear in one single photo. He always went with one of his mates who were never in them either. I used to ask him why he never snapped his friend in front of the Hollywood sign or on the Vegas Strip, or why his friend never took his photo. He would just shrug and say neither of them liked having their picture taken. I think my dad's probably to blame for that, forcing him to pose, pointing at inanimate objects with the rest of the family when he was little. I think he could have been in some cracking photos though. I can picture it in my head. My brother, aged thirty-two, pointing at the Grand Canyon while wearing his bus driver's hat.

Frank and Sheila, meanwhile had become international 'jet setters'. They had been to Benidorm with their best friends Terence (almost hanging out of the closet door now) and his (still oblivious wife, Marjorie). They had the time of their lives over there and from then on, they went abroad regularly, looking down their noses at my parents who were still holidaying in Scarborough or Great Yarmouth. They gave up their holiday home in the country (caravan in a field) and concentrated on getting as orange and wrinkly as was humanly possible up and down the Costa del Sol.

One time when they were going they asked us to take them to Leeds/Bradford Airport.

That was asking for trouble really with my husband's sense of direction and refusal to believe maps and signposts. Once again, we got hopelessly lost and when we eventually got them there it was with minutes to spare before the check in closed. We had to pick them up again when they arrived back but we were more successful the second time and actually got there a bit early. We were waiting in arrivals for them to come through and when they did we almost died of embarrassment. Everyone else seemed quite normal, just happy holiday makers in summer clothes with nice, golden tans. Then Frank and Sheila came staggering through, half drunk, bright lobster red, wearing massive sombreros and carrying a three-foot donkey each. It was quite a squash in the car going home.

After their first trip with Terence and Marjorie we were all invited to view the holiday snaps. Frank, as ever had to show off so instead of just handing the photos around he had rigged up a projector and set up chairs for a viewing. It was riveting. Snapshot after snapshot of Frank, Sheila, Terence and Marjorie in a variety of bars, topless on the beach (yuk) and dancing around with cocktails stuffed with umbrellas, sparklers and god knows what else.

As we watched the show it soon became apparent that something was happening to Terence, he seemed to be coming out a bit more in every photo. His hair got bigger, his clothes got brighter and by day four he seemed to be wearing a lady's blouse and a sarong. Marjorie's expression in the photos seemed to be changing along with her husband's transformation. You could see that, frame by frame the penny was starting to drop. I had an inkling that we probably wouldn't be getting an invitation to their next wedding anniversary party. Oh well, one less Christmas card on the list.

CHAPTER FOUR

Bitchy Baby Club

Now that my daughter was six months old I was practically an old hand at this mothering game. I never once came home from the shops without her, though I did once walk past my poor dog, tied up outside the shop and whimpering as he watched me go home without him. To be fair I did remember him after a few hours and went back for him although he never looked at me in the same way again and always ran under the couch whenever I shouted him for walkies.

I also never turned her legs blue again either, though by now her thighs were so big it wouldn't have been hard. Let's just say her pants needed lots of leg room. For such a tiny scrap of a baby she had astounded all the midwives by piling on the pounds and now weighed a stone. I had muscles like Popeye from lugging her around. Because of this we were 'invited' to attend more baby clinics than usual. I think we were really at baby weightwatchers, but nobody would admit to this.

My mother was very annoyed at everyone poking their noses in and inferring that she had a fat granddaughter. She wanted to come with us to assure them that our family were very aware of what 'healthy eating' meant. I absolutely refused her on this one. If she started telling them how she had brought a family up almost entirely on lard I would be done for, I would probably still be under supervision to this day. Even today, her idea of 'five a day' means five different flavoured jelly babies and the only fruit she eats is hidden away in the bottom of her daily trifle.

Besides, we were only just starting on solid foods. Mind you, when I say 'solid' most of my daughter's food looked the same in the jar as it did in her nappy a few hours later. I think she was just making up for lost time, I knew she would be ok once she started growing a bit more and moving around better.

Nevertheless, we had to go every few weeks to be 'monitored' by more bitchy midwives who thought they knew better, even though hardly any of them had kids. I once asked one of them if she had any children and she visibly shuddered as if I'd just asked if she had a nasty bladder infection.

If I thought the midwives were bitchy though, they had nothing on the other mothers. Everyone in the clinic thought they had the most beautiful, most advanced, intelligent baby in the place. Some of them were beautiful (not as beautiful as mine but still beautiful), but some of them had very unfortunate faces. I began to understand the saying 'a face only a mother could love' a bit more after a few visits to this place. The mothers were very nice to each other's faces and they would coo over each other's babies' non-stop. That was until one of them was called through into the other room, then the bitch fest would begin in earnest.

"Oh, my god, did you see the ears on that?"

"I wouldn't like to peer into that one's cot in the middle of the night."

"That reminds me, did anyone see 'The Elephant Man' on the telly last week?"

They were so cruel it wasn't true. I had always imagined it to be like this backstage at a Miss World contest, I didn't expect to hear things like this in a baby clinic. Thank god, I hadn't brought my mother, with her knack for insulting people without even trying we would have been lynched in this place.

Whenever we were called through I would try and stand near the door to see if I could hear them talking about us. If I ever heard anyone say anything about thunder thighs there would be hell to pay.

As well as judging each other's offspring by their appearance, they were all also in competition to see whose child was advancing the fastest. They would all ask each other:

"Is yours trying to stand yet?"

"Can yours hold a cup yet?"

"Can yours feed him/herself yet?"

The ones that weren't quite there yet were all treated to sympathetic looks as if they were complete simpletons who would never make it out of nappies. Then they would all start bragging for an hour about the things their little darlings had achieved already.

"Well my Miranda can crawl forwards and backwards and get up the stairs already."

"My Jason can sing along with all my favourite songs."

"My Katherine can already say five sentences and she's only nine months."

At this we would all look at Katherine, waiting for her to astound us with her vocabulary but she would just sit, slack jawed and drooling, trying to see how far she could get her fingers up her nose as her mother pointed out, she was 'shy'.

On and on it went, everyone trying to outdo the last whopping great lie. They must have been lying. either that or sitting in this clinic were the most advanced group of children ever known to man.

I always got out of there as quickly as I could, they were a horrible bunch of women. Besides, we had to get back, my daughter had a piano concerto to finish composing before she went to bed to finish reading 'War and Peace'.

For the last three months, we had been living in our own little house. We couldn't manage in our flat anymore so when my daughter was three months old we packed up and moved across town and now lived about a twenty-minute walk from my parents' house. That meant we were there a few times a week so that my mother and Joan from next door could spoil the baby while I put my feet up and read the papers. Friday afternoons we always walked to my Aunty Dolly's and spent a few hours gossiping and eating biscuits.

We now had a massive garden which was still a bit of a wilderness as we had no clue about gardening. My dad would have loved a garden that big and he was always trying to convince us to do things with vegetable patches and compost heaps. For the time being we had cut the grass in a small area for the little one to play in and left the rest to Mother Nature. We would think again after winter.

A few weeks before this we had been given some news. Cheryl and Alistair had evidently overcome whatever the 'problem' was when they had first got married and now they were expecting in a few months' time. We were now awaiting the arrival of another little cousin. I could only shudder at the thought of what this poor baby would be dressed in judging by the things she had knitted for the other two babies over the last year. Until I had seen some of her creations it had never crossed my mind that you could dress a three-month old baby girl in khaki. I hadn't even realised that you could buy khaki coloured wool. I had always thought my mother was the world's maddest knitter but she had obviously handed over her crown.

When I had first met Cheryl at the shop were we both worked she seemed quite normal, I didn't quite know what had happened to her. Since getting married she had turned practically overnight into a middle-aged woman and she was still only twenty. One of the first things she did after she was married was to buy a yellow, nylon overall, the sort that you see old ladies or school cleaners wearing. She would put this on every day to do the housework along with rubber gloves. There were only two of them in a little flat, how bad could it possibly be that you needed rubber gloves and overalls to clean it. Since we had both been sacked from the shop four years before, she had moved on to work in a paint and plastics factory. I could only think the fumes must have addled her brain.

We had just had our first family Christmas with the three of us. Our daughter had been given dozens of presents which, on opening, turned out to be teddies, rabbits, pandas and every other animal that anyone ever thought would make a good soft toy. By the time we were finished opening them we could have opened a stall on a fairground. I started to think we might have to move again to give them all an extra bedroom.

We had spent Christmas afternoon at my parents and Boxing Day afternoon at Frank and Sheila's. Anne had brought her little daughter who was nearly eleven months old by then and we had great fun dressing both babies up when they had fallen asleep. We all fell about laughing at the sight of them both, propped up on pillows snoring their little heads off. Each one was wearing a plastic moustache and a paper hat out of the Christmas Crackers and they both had a cigar in one hand and a glass of whisky in the other.

Of course, we had to take photos of them dressed up like this to embarrass them both when they were sixteen. My mother said we were cruel but those were always my favourite baby pictures. Besides, over the coming years we took plenty that were a lot worse.

CHAPTER FIVE

Royal Weddings and Yodelling Grandads

Unbelievably a year had passed and it was our daughter's first birthday. We couldn't believe how fast it had gone. The little scrap of a thing that we had brought home from the hospital was now walking around the place like she'd been doing it for years. Now that she could get around on two legs the thunder thighs had disappeared and now she looked like the other toddlers, just a bit more petite. We knew she was never going to be a giant as I was only five feet three and her dad only five feet seven. We were destined to be a family of short arses. She didn't actually crawl until after she had started walking, before that she had just sort of bum shuffled and rolled herself around to get to where she wanted to be. My mother said she didn't look very dignified throwing herself around the carpet. I asked her when she had last seen a dignified baby, I had certainly never seen one and anyway, compared to a lot of the snotty, dribbling, sick covered ones I had seen at the baby clinics I thought she was positively ladylike.

Now that she was walking, every time we went to my parent's house my brother had a panic attack. He was eleven now and trying desperately to keep his niece's sticky little fingers away from all his things. My dad was still trying to convince him to be a bus driver and his model bus collection was getting bigger by the day. Because they were all brightly coloured and had spinny things on them she was drawn to them and he spent many a happy hour trying to wrestle them from her vice like grip. For a one year, old she was quite strong and they would have quite a tussle before my mother would step in to sort it out. I used to sit back and watch, it was very entertaining.

My dad was forever dumping her onto my brother's knee for a 'photo with Uncle'. On all these photos his expression is priceless, he looks so uncomfortable bless him. He looks as if he has just sat in something unspeakable but he's the only one that knows about it.

I was dreading her opening her presents in case everybody had bought her stuffed toys again, we had dozens of them already. Luckily most people had bought her activity toys that had brightly coloured buttons and switches and things and made squeaky noises. My brother seemed to enjoy these too.

He had given up Avon collecting these days. Now that he was eleven my mother could leave him at home alone on the days she couldn't convince him to go to school. Her excuse to my dad had always been that she had to take him with her. She had dropped a few hints over the last few months about how a cute baby might convince more people not to slam their doors in her face but I put my foot down on that idea. I was not going to 'pimp' my daughter out just so my mother could sell a few more bottles of bubble bath.

On her birthday, we went to spend some time with her older cousin. She was only five months older but that five months made a big difference, she had done everything first so she thought that gave her the right to throw her weight around. If my daughter picked up a toy she would immediately decide that was the toy that she wanted and there would be a mad tug of war between them which usually descended into violence. They would end up pushing or slapping each other which always ended in tears until they were separated. Every photo we tried to take of the two happy little cousins together always looked the same. Two big red faces with puffy eyes, still trying to elbow each other out of the way to be at the front of the picture. To say what a bad start they had they get on really well nowadays.

A few weeks before her birthday our family had expanded again when Cheryl gave birth to a baby boy with the longest legs anyone had ever seen on a baby. Bless him he looked like a new-born giraffe, nobody knew who he had got these legs from but we all knew his Moses basket wouldn't be any good for more than a week or so, unless Cheryl cut the end out of it. He was also destined to grow up into the world's clumsiest child, he could walk into a shop and things would just fall off shelves and topple over, it was like he had some sort of inbuilt magnet that would attract things to him. None of us would ever take him shopping if we could avoid it, it was too embarrassing though his long legs did come in useful when it came to running away from irate shopkeepers. I have to admit to feeling a bit smug when I saw his legs. In my eyes this was payback for all those times Cheryl had poked my daughter's thighs laughing:

"Look at them, they don't even wobble, they're solid."

Maybe they had been solid but at least I had never had to cut the feet off her baby grow.

We never tried to take his photo with his cousins in the early days, it was too risky. The way they fought over everything they were likely to go for a leg each and go into their usual tug of war. He would have enough to deal with when he got older, he didn't need displaced testicles to add to his worries.

Whenever we visited my husband's side of the family we always stopped off last at his nanna and grandad's house. They were really nice, Nanna was everything you wanted your nanna to be, a proper old lady, handing out sweets and checking to see if you were wearing your vest. Unfortunately, Grandad wasn't doing as well, he had recently misplaced some of his marbles and was driving Nanna to distraction.

He had always kept pigeons in a small loft in the garden, it kept him occupied and out of the house which pleased Nanna as he wasn't under her feet. It was the perfect hobby for him. Now however, he had a new hobby, one which none of us saw coming, it was yodelling. This was hysterically funny to everyone else but Nanna was at the end of her tether. He didn't just yodel in the garden, to his pigeons, that would have been bad enough. No, he yodelled indoors, very loudly, and to top it off he made tape recordings of himself yodelling, to make sure he got it just right. He would yodel for a while, then play it back to see how it sounded, if he noticed bits that could be improved he would start over, yodelling into the tape recorder. Then he would play it back again and the whole process would continue over and over.

Nobody knew where this new obsession had sprung up from, he had never yodelled before. He had always enjoyed singing and had been known to record himself doing that but this was a whole new thing. He would still sing a lot of the same old songs as before but now with added yodelling, it was baffling.

We could hear him as soon as we got out of the car at the top of their little block of houses, it sounded like a cat choking on bagpipes, it was hysterical. Nanna was hysterical as well but in a different way, she was going out of her mind with it all. We would go in to say hello to him and he would stop yodelling long enough to greet us and tell my daughter what a big boy she was getting, then he would get back to his 'recording'. He would try and convince us to take one of his tapes with us to play in the car but we always politely declined.

Sometimes, to give poor Nanna a break we took him to the park for a nice bit of fresh air. We had to stop doing this when one day he climbed over a fence, whipped out a garden trowel and started digging up plants from the displays to put in his garden. Thank god this was before CCTV, I had spent enough time in court already.

I had started to think that maybe my family wasn't as strange as I had always thought. After all, here was Cheryl, a far madder knitter and colour coordinator than my mother had ever been and now here was Grandad, stealing the title of 'World's Worst Warbler' from my mother. Over the years, I had heard a lot of strange sounds coming from the kitchen but nothing like this. Even all those months when she and Joan next door were accompanied by the dog howling along with their harmonies didn't compare to this. Maybe I had been wrong all these years and I hadn't been so different after all, maybe everyone's family was as bad, either that or it was just my natural knack for attracting nutters.

Just after my daughter's birthday came the biggest event in Britain for years, The Royal Wedding. Prince Charles was finally getting married and the people who decide these things had picked out Lady Diana Spencer to be his bride (brood mare). The world had been going mad ever since it had been announced and no matter where you went there was no escaping it. There were tea towels with their faces plastered on them, mugs, key rings, commemorative plates, you name it, if it existed someone had found a way to stick them on it. We had never had any interest in the Royal family in my house growing up and it was no different now. My mother said she couldn't care less and wouldn't be bothered even turning the telly on to watch it.

I was only interested because I wanted to see the dress, newsreaders had been banging on about it for months, talking to designers and trying to figure out how much it was actually costing. On the day of the wedding I put my daughter in her buggy and we walked round to my Aunty Dolly's house to watch it there. She didn't like the Royal family any more than the rest of us but she also wanted to see a dress that cost more than all of our houses put together and then some.

On the way there we passed several street parties that were already under way, everyone had hung red, white and blue bunting everywhere and every other little girl seemed to be dressed as Lady Di. It looked like the whole town had gone bonkers. We settled down to watch in front of Aunty Dolly's telly and waited for it to begin. When they wheeled the bride out in the carriage we oohed and aahed at the tiara and the coach, but we couldn't really see much of the dress as she seemed to be all squashed up in there. When the carriage pulled up outside the Abbey we waited for her to get out and show off this hideously expensive dress that everyone had been speculating about for months. When she actually stepped out we were gobsmacked. Not only was it hideously expensive, it was hideous full stop, it looked like a giant crumpled dish rag. My Aunty Dolly wanted to know why the hell nobody had ironed it and I was just thinking that at last I had seen a wedding dress uglier than my own. What a let-down.

We turned it off after that as it was just boring and we only watched the bit on the balcony when the boring bits had finished. On the way home, we stopped off at my mother's for a quick brew. For someone who wasn't interested in the wedding and said she wouldn't be bothered watching it she seemed to know a lot about it.

Today it's a different story. After the disaster that the Royal marriage became in later years, my mother decided to hate Prince Charles with a vengeance. She blames him for ruining that poor girl's life and having her bumped off so he could marry 'that sour faced trollop'. She will not have the name 'Camilla' spoken in her house and calls Charles 'that big eared prat', it's so funny.

Sometimes I will ask if her if she saw Camilla on the news and tell her she looked ever so nice, her lips purse up tighter than a duck's bum and I can feel her eyes boring into my head, giving me her 'death stare'. Once I even went as far as telling her Diana was as 'mad as a box of frogs anyway', she went ballistic, I thought she was going to choke on her Werther's Original. If she could have moved faster I might have been in trouble. I know I'm never in any serious danger from my mother though, she needs me too much to cause me bodily harm and if I ever get worried I just pull the plug out of her electric recliner chair. I can leave her stuck reclining for hours until she calms down. You see when we bought it I 'forgot' to put in the back up battery.

CHAPTER SIX

Whoops, I Did It Again

My husband had lately given up the building trade for a while and was now a delivery driver. He had several different routes including one that kept him in our area. On the days he was in the neighbourhood he would often pop home for a wee, his bladder being still the size of a peanut. One day when he was really bursting and couldn't wait until he got home he parked his lorry up and went into the gent's toilets that were situated near the shops in our area.

Now I had lived in this area since I was nine years old and around here we had always known about these toilets. It was well known that they only existed to give all the local perverts somewhere to hang out (literally) and get their jollies. Unfortunately, it had never crossed my mind to tell my husband about them. He went in there quite innocently thinking he could have a quick wee in peace and then go on with his day. He managed to make it into a cubicle (he always preferred a cubicle if there was one) and was mid wee before the first pervert struck. To his horror, the door started to open, he shouted that there was someone in there but whoever was outside took this as an invitation to come in and join the party. The door kept opening so he did his best to kick it shut, being mid wee he couldn't stop long enough to turn around and close it properly.

He carried on shouting (and swearing) to let the weirdo outside know in no uncertain terms that he wasn't in the mood for a get together. This just gave whoever it was the idea that he was playing hard to get and the door kept opening. Finally, he finished his wee just as the door was opened again, this time he kicked it so hard it smacked the person outside hard in the face knocking them down. My husband ran out to tackle him and was quite surprised to find three new friends waiting for him to come out and play. They had brought their own 'toys' with them and were already playing while they waited.

Not wanting to stay and play Twister with three big perverts he swung a few kicks and punches and legged it back to his lorry. He had only gone a few yards up the road before he spotted a policeman so he stopped him to report the 'incident'. You can imagine his surprise when the policeman started laughing.

"What did you want to go in there for?" He asked him.

"A pee, what do you think I went in there for?"

The policeman then went on to tell him what these toilets were really for, he was quite amused. He said everyone round here knew that. And that was that, he told him not to go in there again if he didn't want to play.

Can you imagine that happening nowadays, the police looking on laughing as unsuspecting men looking for a quick innocent wee were ceremoniously gang raped opposite Tesco's. The policeman was quite helpful though, he reeled off a list of other toilets to avoid on his rounds if he didn't want a repeat performance.

My husband couldn't believe it. He drove straight home to tell me what had happened, I should have at least acted shocked I suppose. Instead I just repeated what the policeman had asked him.

"What did you want to go in there for?" He was horrified when he realised that I had known all along about the toilets. He wanted to know why, in all the times we had walked or driven by them that it had never once crossed my mind to tell him about them. I told him I had never thought about it, I wasn't a tour guide. I left it to my mother to announce things as we passed them. Now if she had been in the car when we went by them that would have been something, I can just hear it now:

"PUBLICCC CONVEENIENCE FORR PERVERRTSS!"

He would certainly have remembered that!

Over the years, he has found himself in a few scrapes but, to be fair to him a lot of them have been my fault, I seem to have a habit of sending him off into situations that wouldn't have happened if I had been paying more attention. One such situation occurred about a year after the toilet fiasco. For a few years now he had suffered with pains in his legs and his doctor decided it might be something to do with his veins. He contacted the local hospital and told us to expect an appointment soon.

A couple of weeks later an appointment card dropped through the door for him. I wrote the time and date down and when the day came around I stuck the card in his pocket and sent him on his way. His appointment was for eleven o clock in the morning, I knew he would probably be a few hours but by four o clock there was still no sign of him. I started to get a bit worried but I knew if they had decided to keep him in for anything then I would have heard.

Around quarter to six I heard him come in. I looked up and saw him standing there with a strange look on his face. When he spoke, he sounded very calm.

"When that appointment card came did you read it?"

"Yes, course I did, why?"

"Did it have my name on it?"

"Course it did, why?"

"Did you see both names, first and last?"

By now I was getting impatient, I had no clue what he was on about.

"I read it, the card was for you, what's up with you?"

"It wasn't for me you stupid woman", he yelled (actually he might not have said "woman"), it was my first name on it but it was a different surname, I have been through hell today."

I had to admit I hadn't really looked at the name properly, he was expecting an appointment so I had just naturally assumed that this was it. It turned out it was for someone else and the addresses had been mixed up. This wouldn't have been so bad had the person the hospital was expecting not been a mental patient. A mental patient suffering from severe paranoid delusions.

When my husband had arrived and presented his appointment card he had been immediately whisked off to a 'special' ward where all the doors locked behind him. Because it was supposed to be a calm, friendly atmosphere the doctors and nurses all called him by his first name (the same name as the real patient) so, at first alarm bells didn't ring for him. When he finally realised something was up and these people weren't interested in looking at his legs he tried to tell them there must have been a mistake made somewhere. Unfortunately, the medical staff thought this was all part of his 'delusions' and paid no attention. The more agitated he got the more they tried to tell him he was just imagining everything. They tried to put him in a 'quiet' room and started ordering different drugs to be administered seeing as they could tell he hadn't been taking his medication. They knew this because they had taken quite a few blood samples by then. He spent the next few hours, refusing all drugs and yelling to anyone in earshot that he was only here 'for his legs'. To calm him down the doctors decided to play along and stuck him on a treadmill, telling him to run until his legs felt tired. For added effect they stuck some wires onto his head.

This went on for ages until someone finally realised that he might not be who they thought he was. Eventually they brought some of his medical records and checked some of his old scars against the records from various accidents and operations he had been through over the years. When they realised their mistake, they apologised profusely and told him he could go home. After he had finished threatening to sue the pants off them he took his leave and came home.

He was beside himself, absolutely furious but I couldn't stop laughing. The madder he got, the more I laughed, I couldn't help it. I could just picture him, dressed in one of those hospital gowns where your bum sticks out the back, wires all over his head, running on a treadmill shouting for somebody to turn it off and look at his legs. To add insult to injury, his legs were aching worse than ever, due to the fact he had been running half the day.

Eventually he saw the funny side (about six years later) and today we sometimes still have a good laugh about it. After that, whenever he got any kind of appointment through the post I always double checked both names and the address to be on the safe side and he always took loads of I.D with him as well, just in case. I still sometimes wonder what happened to the real person that should have been there though. Did he also make the same mistake and turn up for the wrong appointment, if so I wonder what he thought when his 'psychiatrist made' him take off his trousers and started poking around at his legs. I suppose it would have made a change from his usual appointments, though it might have given him a whole new thing to be paranoid about.

I've a feeling that could probably be my fault as well.

CHAPTER SEVEN

Birthday Blues

It was now December 1981 and coming up to my twenty first birthday. My daughter was almost eighteen months now and as well as walking she was also starting to talk. Rubbish mostly but she looked like she knew what she was on about. She loved going to my parents at this time of year as my dad went mental with the Christmas decorations. He was still insisting on a real tree so that meant when she had been there for a few hours she would be secreting little pine needles all over. When she had her bath before bed she would clog the plughole with loads of the bloody things as they floated out from every orifice. I was still trying to persuade my dad to switch to a fake tree but it would be a few more years before he actually gave in.

For now, he was still insisting on the real deal which meant by Christmas day there would be a sorry looking, half bald specimen standing forlornly in the corner (the tree, not my dad). Not that you could really see the tree that much anyway. Over the years since I was little my parents had been collecting Christmas ornaments and were by now going for the Guinness Book of Records title of 'Most Christmas Ornaments That Can Be Crammed onto A Tree at Once'.

They had never grasped the concept 'less is more' so they just heaped as many onto each branch as they could manage. As well as the ornaments, they had about twenty-seven different sets of lights of all shapes, sizes and colours, luckily, this was before todays, modern flashing and twinkling lights. If they had been around then I'm sure we would have all been sent into epileptic shock every time they were switched on.

As if the lights and ornaments weren't enough they would then pile around three or four boxes of Christmas Crackers and god knows how many chocolates on as well and then finish the whole lot off with a giant fairy perched on the very top. I don't know where they got the fairy from but she was a big girl. By the time she was in place, spread eagled on the topmost branch you could practically hear the tree begging for mercy. It was so heavy my dad used to tie it to the wall to stop it from toppling over. It was a sight to behold.

I was a little worried about my upcoming birthday. For years now I had been listening to my mother telling me the story of how she came to be a 'big girl' herself. Apparently, on her wedding day she had been an eight-stone slip of a thing. Fast forward a year and she had become a twelve-stone slip of a thing. She swore this was nothing to do with over eating, she said everything just happened when she turned twenty-one, overnight she just 'ballooned'.

She said I would find out how it felt when my birthday came around, she was sure it would happen to me as well. Now I knew this was impossible but in the back of my mind I was still terrified, what if she was right and our family had some genetic defect? After all, we were defective in most other areas.

The night before my birthday I undressed for bed, wondering if my clothes would still fit me in the morning. I don't know who was more worried, me or my husband. He warned me that if something happened to me in the night I was to stay on my own side of the bed so that he was in no danger of getting squashed.

When my birthday morning rolled around I opened one eye and peeled the covers back slowly. To my great relief, I was the same size I had been the night before, I knew this would annoy my mother no end. She would finally have to admit that maybe her size had something to do with the vast quantities of food that she shovelled into her face on a daily basis.

Over the years, I had watched her try many different diets. She joined many of those slimming clubs where she would go to meetings every week to be publicly weighed and humiliated. They never lasted long. She would start out full of good intentions, eating salads and cottage cheese but after a few days she would slide back into her old habits. For a time, she bought and wore bigger, stronger 'all in ones', the type of underwear that holds everything in and gives the wearer the appearance of being smaller. The trouble with those were that when you squeeze all that excess 'everything' into one place it has to try and escape somewhere else. She just ended up with most of herself popping out above and below the underwear, giving her a very odd appearance. It was hard to tell where her bosom ended and her chins began.

When Slim-fast first came onto the market she thought her prayers had been answered, a meal that looked like a milkshake. The idea was to have a healthy breakfast, a shake for lunch and a healthy evening meal. However, my mother's idea was to have whatever she liked for breakfast dinner and tea and accompany each meal with the healthy shake. This meant she actually went from three meals a day to six. Unsurprisingly she put more weight on and went around telling everyone not to bother buying Slim-fast as it was rubbish and didn't work. She was completely bonkers.

For a short time in the early eighties her doctor gave her slimming tablets, these were basically amphetamines and they worked. They curbed her appetite and stopped her eating so much, she actually began to lose weight. Unfortunately, they also stopped her sleeping or sitting still. For the first time since I had known her she began to throw herself into housework, the only trouble was she would start before the rest of the household woke up.

She was up, cleaning windows at six in the morning and hoovering everywhere she could reach. My dad was fed up of his plate being snatched from under his nose to be washed before he'd even finished half of his meal and if he and my brother stayed in one place too long they would end up getting dusted and polished. Also, she talked nonstop, about anything and everything, she drove us all nuts, even my daughter would stay in her buggy when we visited and pretend to be asleep so that she would leave her alone. Even at that young age there's a limit to how many times you want to be piggy backed around the garden by your Grandma on a speed trip.

Eventually she burnt herself out, she couldn't keep going at that pace. My dad persuaded her to stop taking the pills and, once they were out of her system she slept for a week and then went back to eating instead of cleaning. She carried on 'dieting' for the next thirty years or so, getting steadily bigger until, finally she stopped caring, stopped weighing herself and got on with the business of eating whatever she fancied. We don't know what she weighs anymore as none of us have any scales big enough for her to fit on.

In contrast, while my mother was one of nature's larger ladies, Sheila was really skinny, she could eat what she liked and still look like a string bean with a frizzy perm. She wasn't happy about being so thin but pretended she was so that she could gloat over my mother and have little digs about her weight. My mother, in turn would make fun of Sheila's chest, calling her bosom two fried eggs on an ironing board. When she heard about Sheila going topless on holiday she said it wouldn't matter who saw her, they would think she was a man anyway. They were worse than kids in the school playground.

Frank and Sheila had just come back from abroad again. They were giving the Costa del Sol a miss for a bit and had started to go further afield on their travels in search of a bit more culture. They had recently been to Mykonos one of the Greek islands. Back then none of us had ever heard of any Greek islands so we were completely unaware that Mykonos was the favourite holiday spot of gay men (you would think Terence might have warned them). Frank and Sheila were also unaware but I think after the first couple of days they started to get an inkling. Sheila loved it and made lots of new fabulous friends, (maybe they thought the same way as my mother and thought she was a gay man too) but Frank wasn't quite as thrilled. None of us are still actually sure what went on over there but apparently, there was a 'dress code' for the men who were looking for a bit of holiday fun. It was something to do with which shoulder you carried your bag or camera on or some such thing. Anyway, there was a bit of a hoo ha one day when Frank went down to the beach carrying his bag on the wrong shoulder and something of a misunderstanding had taken place. They both refused to discuss it no matter how many times we tried to get it out of them so eventually we gave up asking.

Whatever happened it was never spoken of again in their house. To add insult to injury, on arrival back in England someone in customs must have thought Frank looked a bit dodgy and after going through his luggage he was taken away for a full body search. That was a touchy subject for a while as well so we never spoke about that either and the next year they went back to Benidorm.

CHAPTER EIGHT

Billy Big Mouth

The summer my daughter turned two was an interesting one. I'm sure there are still a few people out there that remember that time too but more on that later. By the time her birthday came around she was talking nonstop. She had gone from one syllable words to complete sentences practically overnight, it sounded so funny. Because we still weren't used to hearing her, every time she spoke we fell about laughing, it drove her mad. She would stand shaking a finger and telling us off,

"Dop it, dop it right now, it not funny."

She was still having a bit of trouble saying 'St' and also hadn't got the hang of 'V' so every morning when she got dressed she always put on her knickers and best.

We were starting to realise that we should have been a bit more careful what we said in front of her. It had been too easy to forget there was a little person sitting there in the buggy taking in everything we said. One such example was brought to light one day when she was staying over with my parents.

Frank and Sheila had some neighbours, Sandra and Bill that they socialised with sometimes. They were a bit loud when they had been drinking, Sheila told us that every time they had all been out together, on the way home Bill would get a bit frisky with Sandra. On arrival at their house he would practically shove her through the front door shouting

"Knickers off, knockers out" (who said romance was dead).

We all used to laugh about this and every time we saw Sandra we would all shout it at her, completely forgetting about little ears flapping.

All was well until she started to talk and to repeat everything she had been keeping stored up in her memory. Overnight it all started to come out. On this occasion, my mother was getting her ready for bed at their house, quite unknowingly she said to her,

"Come on, knickers off."

You can imagine how surprised and delighted she was when her beautiful innocent little granddaughter shouted back at her,

"Knockers out."

I got quite a telling off about that one the next morning. My mother said she had already been through all this once when my brother was that age. Then he had embarrassed her every time she took him shopping by calling all his fellow shoppers pigs and buggers, she said she wasn't going through all that again and if I wanted her to babysit I had better clean up my daughter's potty mouth.

Other than that delightful little saying though, she wasn't too bad in public. As she got a bit older she did take great delight in embarrassing me on buses though, I swear she did it on purpose. She would wait until there was a lull in the conversation and then pipe up,

"Mammy, how does electric work?"

All eyes would immediately swivel towards me, waiting for me to astound them all with my knowledge. No mobile phones or Google in those days.

"I'll explain it when we get home", I would tell her but this wasn't good enough.

"I want to know now." she would insist.

"There isn't time now, we're nearly home."

"No, we're not, its ages yet, tell me now."

"Your dad will tell you all about it."

"I want you to tell me."

By now, half the bus wanted me to tell her as well, I could see them all settling in for a good laugh.

I would usually get out of these situations by shoving sweets into her ever-open mouth.

"Here you are sweetheart, let's see how many jelly babies we can cram into your mouth at once shall we, that'll be fun won't it?"

She probably wouldn't have agreed with me on that one but it was hard for her to tell me when her cheeks were bulging like a hamster and little heads and feet were poking out of her mouth. At least that would buy me enough time to get her off the bus without further embarrassment.

On one occasion when we were on the bus though she managed to embarrass me a lot more than that. We were going into town and had stopped at the terminus to wait for more passengers. We had to wait for about ten minutes so the driver had turned off the engine and it was really quiet, there were only about six of us on the bus. Suddenly my daughter started whispering in my ear, I couldn't understand a word of what she was going on about.

"Speak up a bit, I can't hear you." I said. Again, she whispered in my ear and again I couldn't hear what she was saying.

"I still can't hear you, say it properly, there's no need to whisper."

To my horror, she pointed straight at the rather large lady sitting dead opposite us and shouted at the top of her voice,

"I SAID ISN'T THAT LADY FAT!"

I didn't know where to put myself, I wanted the ground to open up and swallow us both. I couldn't even pretend that she was talking about someone else as she was pointing straight at the poor woman. All I could do was tell her not to be so rude, you didn't say things like that about people.

"I know that." said my daughter, "That's why I was whispering."

It seemed like every time we got on a bus in those days I always had a red face by the time we got off again. One day when it was quiet on the bus she did a really loud burp. Now in the last two years or so she must have done hundreds of burps but this was the first time she had ever really taken any notice. Her eyes grew wide with astonishment, she looked up at me in complete surprise and announced to half the bus,

"Ooh, I pumped out me face."

Everyone fell about laughing at her, asking each other, "Did you hear that?"

I realised that day that I had a bit of a comedian on my hands. To this day, even though she's in her thirties now, whenever she does a burp, we all say,

"Pumping out your face again?"

She also took to entertaining crowds at bus stops and in queues by singing and dancing.

Little old ladies would clap and give her sweets which only encouraged her. For a while

I worried that she had inherited my mother's 'entertainment gene', I didn't think I could go through all that again. Luckily the phase passed and the rest of us breathed a sigh of relief.

By this time, we had just been joined by another cousin, Anne had recently given birth to another gorgeous little girl with big dark eyes and curly dark hair she looked like a cute little bush baby and she was really beautiful. On her first meeting with her new cousin my daughter had pulled the dummy from her own mouth and clinked it against the one in the baby's mouth.

"Cheers." she pronounced.

Sometimes I was baffled by the things she did. We had taken her dummies away just before she turned two, telling her she was a big girl now and didn't need them anymore. Unfortunately, she had foreseen this event and had taken to stashing secret supplies all over the house. Just when I thought I had found and disposed of the last one she would appear with another one sticking out of her face. She finally gave them up when my dad showed her how to suck her thumb instead (thanks for that) and then it took another year to get her to give up this new habit. After all, you can take dummies away from a child but you're not allowed to remove their thumbs.

Cheryl wasn't so kind on meeting her new little niece, she laughed that she looked like a little monkey. I was beginning to see a new side to Cheryl, where our children were concerned she seemed to have a cruel streak. When my daughter started teething her front teeth came in at different times, the first one was halfway grown when the other one came through. This meant that for a few months she had one front tooth a bit longer than the other. For some reason, Cheryl thought that this made her look like Mr Humphries from the TV comedy 'Are you being served'. Every time my daughter smiled at her she would go into hysterical laughter, shouting "I'm Free!" There was really no need for it.

I could have been just as cruel if I wanted but I couldn't bring myself to pick on innocent children. I would look across at Geoffrey the Giraffe sitting in his high chair, feet scraping the floor and bite my tongue. It wasn't his fault his mother had a bitchy streak.

He was trying to walk by this time but, bless him it wasn't easy. He already had the inbuilt clumsiness, add to that his three-foot long spaghetti legs and it was a recipe for disaster, he always ended up in a heap on the floor with his legs wrapped around each other like a liquorice twist. We all knew that when he did finally get the hang of it he would attract some attention. To start with he was twice the height of most other toddlers, if he kept going at this rate he would be almost as tall as his mother by the time he turned two, as well as this, because she was so scared of losing him she kept him in reins every time they went out. He had some white ones with little bunny rabbits on them, unfortunately from a distance it looked like he was wearing a bra. When the day came that he finally mastered the art of walking I could only imagine the looks the pair of them were going to get around the shops.

A giant toddler with legs like a supermodel, tottering around on a leash while wearing a Wonderbra. It didn't bear thinking about.

As I mentioned at the start of this chapter, that summer would turn out to be a memorable one. We were still trying to get to grips with our huge garden, we had a lawn mower but it was still a never-ending job plus there were loads of bushes and hedges all over the place. Everything seemed to grow twice as fast as we could cut it.

One afternoon I came back from shopping with my daughter to find my husband pleased as punch. He said he had bought something which would soon get all our gardening problems sorted, I assumed he had bought us a new lawnmower, maybe even one of those that you sat on. I rushed out into the back garden to have a look. His new purchase wasn't a lawnmower, not even a new push one, his new purchase was Billy.

Billy was a goat. Just as his name suggested he was a Billy goat, a big white thing with horns. To his credit, he had made a good start on the garden, half of the grass was really short now and he was just making a start on the bushes at the back. I couldn't believe what I was seeing, I was speechless. My daughter however was delighted, she was already unfastening the straps of her buggy to go and see him. She was just like her dad for animals, they loved any sort of animal, bird, fish, insect or reptile. We had noticed this from a very early age. One of the first things she did when she started walking was to pluck a sparrow from a hedge in Frank and Sheila's garden and bring it indoors. My dad called her Dr Doolittle.

Sheila was horrified that my husband had passed this on to his daughter, she still told the tale of the day she had opened his wardrobe door to find an owl sitting in there staring back at her. And she still shuddered about the time a mouse had gone through a hole in his coat pocket and run around inside the lining until they cut it out. She warned me I didn't know what I was in for. I didn't really mind.

It turned out that Billy was a sweetheart, really gentle, he loved to be petted and stroked and was just like a big dog really. By this time, we had acquired a few animals already, we had an old German Shepherd dog called Sherry, a ginger tom cat with a broken tail called Ziggy Stardust (we were David Bowie fans), and a chicken called Clara that came from somewhere I can't even remember now. They all got on like a house on fire and Billy fitted in straight away. We had a porch outside the back door with two big dog baskets in it. Sherry the dog slept with Clara the chicken in one bed, Billy claimed the other one and slept in it with Ziggy the cat. It was an unusual living arrangement but they all seemed to like it.

All the other children in the street loved Billy as well, we fitted him with one of the dog's old collars and the kids would come and put a lead on him and take him for walks up and down the street. Billy loved it and would even let the little ones ride on his back. He became quite a familiar sight in our street. He was doing a great job of keeping the garden well-trimmed as well, we just had to make sure not to leave anything we really liked outside and to keep the washing line high enough that he couldn't reach the clothes. He would literally eat anything.

One afternoon we all came back from a day out and went out to the back garden. The dog, cat and chicken were all there but there was no sign of Billy. We checked up and down the garden in a panic looking for him but he was gone. Then we noticed two things, the first was a Billy shaped hole in the fence where he had eaten through and escaped, the second was a note through the door from the police. The note was informing us that they had our goat in custody and would we please report to the police station to bail him out. My husband jumped straight in the car and went off in search of our wayward goat, when he got there he was met by quite a sight.

Billy was lying on the floor in a police cell with his legs tied together, he looked very sorry for himself. The policeman on duty said he had been picked up at someone's property around a mile from our house. My husband said he was surprised he had gone so far from home to which the policeman replied he probably wasn't half as surprised as the homeowner had been when Billy had crashed through his patio window and landed behind his telly.

Apparently, Billy had ended up in this man's garden, caught sight of himself in the reflection from the windows and had charged. Once through the glass he had become entangled in the wires behind the TV and quite a wrestling match had taken place between Billy and the man who five minutes before had been having forty winks on the couch after his Sunday dinner. Meanwhile the lady of the house had jumped up on the couch and began screaming for help. Their neighbours had heard the commotion and, thinking someone was being murdered had called the police. Billy had been arrested ten minutes later and taken into custody, he was carted off in the back of a police van, tied up with the hysterical woman's washing line. Because he was wearing our dog's old collar with her old I.D tag they were able to find out where he lived.

My husband was mortified but everyone in the station seemed to find it quite funny, they said it made a change from the usual police stuff. Even the poor homeowner saw the funny side once he had calmed down and had a few stiff drinks. He said he wouldn't take things any further as long as we paid for his broken window, which we did. Billy was bailed out and brought home, quite unaware of the chaos and the expense he had caused. He trotted off up the garden and resumed munching the hedges as if none of it had ever happened.

After that Billy's days were numbered. He had tasted freedom now and was no longer content to stay, grazing away in the garden. He took every opportunity to try and break through the fence and it wasn't fair to keep him chained up. After a week or so he went off to live on a farm and we went back to struggling up and down the garden pushing the lawnmower. I have often wondered over the years if he met any of my old pets on the farm. After all, every pet I had ever owned had ended up at the farm as soon as my mother had got fed up of them. I came to the conclusion over the years that this farm must be a pretty big place.

CHAPTER NINE

It's A Steal

All those months when I had been pregnant, and in the first year of my daughter's life everyone seemed to tell me the same thing.

"Make the most of it while she's little, it flies by."

I would just laugh it off but now I was starting to realise they were all right, the time just whizzed by. Nowadays I find myself telling everyone with a baby the same thing, it's like 'blink and you'll miss it'. Good God, I'm old.

It seemed no time at all since I had been arguing with Dr Patronising at the hospital and convincing myself that I was having a one-legged baby. Now it was nearly her third birthday, she was a proper person now with ideas and opinions of her own, sometimes too many opinions. She was also about to get another cousin to add to the clan, Cheryl was about to have another little boy in a few weeks. We didn't know then but he would be born with his legs facing the wrong way and would need several operations in the first year of his life. He turned out perfectly fine but it made me think, what was it with our family and legs. Firstly, my daughter was born pretending she only had the one, then Cheryl's first child had legs like a flamingo and now this. It must have been something in the genes. My mother said it was Frank and Sheila's fault, there were no legs in our side of the family.

My old bridesmaid/schoolfriend Vicky had recently had a little girl as well. When she was a few weeks old we decided that some photos were in order. There was a special offer on in one of the big stores in town so we dressed both of our daughters in their finery and set off on the bus. Vicky had bought a very fancy buggy with all the bells and whistles, it was a lot more complicated than the one that I'd had (my daughter was no longer in a buggy due to the fact that her dad had taken her 'scrambling' across a field in hers and buckled it beyond all recognition). It took us ages to get it all folded up to get on the bus, it was like something out of the Krypton Factor, I was glad mine hadn't been like that, it would have taken us twice as long to get anywhere. All the while we were struggling with it the rest of the passengers on the bus were rolling their eyes and tutting at us although none of them offered their assistance.

We arrived in town and got off the bus, unfolded the Rolls Royce of the buggy world and plonked the baby in it for the short walk to the department store. This was the same store where my mother had spent many a happy hour whacking my brother's behind in front of her fellow shoppers. Every time I came to this shop I would remember their many altercations with a smile on my face. Ah, happy childhood memories, I could picture it as though it were yesterday, my mother's face, purple from the exertion of trying to whack my brother's backside while he lay limp on the ground pretending to be passed out. Happy days.

In recent years, it became a lot harder for my mother to land a slap on his bum. She would still go for her usual standard move, one hand grabbing the back of the neck while swinging the other at the nether region. After my brother got taller and older though he had learnt the same thing that had occurred to me all those years ago, it's harder to hit a moving target. So instead of his old usual trick of going limp so that she would lose her grip and drop him, he would try to run. My mother would keep her grasp on his neck but would be forced to run with him. Because her legs were so short she could never quite keep up and so her swinging arm would hit nothing but the air just behind his ever-moving backside. It was very entertaining to watch, they could still draw quite a crowd once they got going properly. I eventually named my brother's new move 'The Running Dodge Slap'. Now he was almost fourteen though he was a lot taller than she was so she had long since stopped slapping him, it was a good job, with all the humiliation he had endured over the years at her hands he was liable to slap her back.

Once me and Vicky and our offspring arrived in the store we were confronted by the escalator. There was no way we could carry the buggy onto it, even between us, it was just too big. She took the baby out and gave her to me to hold while she tried to fold the buggy up again. She should have practiced more before venturing out in public with it, she really didn't have much of a clue. I gave my daughter my bag to hold and told her to stay put next to me while I tried to assist Vicky. It wasn't easy with a baby under one arm but eventually it was folded up again and we were ready to go up to the next floor. I turned to my daughter to get my bag back from her only to find she was no longer standing next to me. My heart dropped into my stomach as instant panic grabbed at me, she had been there a second ago, how could she have had time to go anywhere. My eyes were trying to scan every inch of the shop floor at once but I couldn't see her anywhere. Just as I was about to faint from sheer terror I heard a little voice from somewhere above my head.

"Look at me I'm riding the stairs."

I looked up and there she was, halfway up the escalator, my handbag clutched in one hand while the other one was giving a regal wave to everyone in the store. She wasn't even holding onto the handrail.

"Oh, my god, what are you doing?" I shouted, though it was quite obvious what she was doing.

"I's off shoppin" she trilled back, completely oblivious to her mother's near heart attack.

"Hold onto the rail." I yelled back at her while I ran up the escalator two steps at a time. I caught up to her just as she neared the top and grabbed her. Because we couldn't get back down we had to carry on to the top and get off. From here I could look down and see Vicky staring back up at me. She couldn't get onto the escalator and follow us as she couldn't manage the baby, the buggy and her bag all at once. In those days, the escalators in our town only went up. Therefore, I had to take my daughter halfway round the store to find the normal staircase back down again. When we got back down and found Vicky we all got back onto the escalator and went back up again, this was taking forever. By the time we got up to the third floor and faffed about getting both girls ready for their photos taking we were exhausted. It was never like this in the old days, then the most we had to worry about was finding the perfect pair of shoes and how much salt and vinegar to put on our lunch time chips. It was quite bewildering how much our lives had changed in the last five years.

Vicky was still enjoying being a new mother and was living in complete ignorance of how her little bundle would turn out in a few years. Her sweet little girl would suddenly morph into a little monster who took great delight in showing Vicky up everywhere they went. When she was really naughty Vicky would give her a little smack but she would turn around and slap Vicky twice as hard and usually in the face. This would then lead to a full-blown fight, she would grab a handful of her mother's hair and pull it so Vicky would pull hers to show her how it felt. They would end up going round in circles in the middle of a shop, each one shouting,

"Let go."

"No, you let go", while other shoppers looked on tutting with disgust and I pretended I didn't know either of them.

One Easter when the little darling was about four she filled the seat of her pants with Cadbury's Cream Eggs and announced to Vicky's visitors that she'd had an 'accident'. Then, another time when Vicky and her husband were getting ready to go out with friends, little sweetheart announced to the friends,

"Mammy won't be long, she's just using Daddy's razor to shave some hair that's sticking out of her knickers."

When she was fifteen they took her abroad for a holiday where she promptly gave them the slip and ended up in a Spanish hospital with alcohol poisoning. Strangely enough, Vicky and her husband Derek never had any other children. They never said why.

In the last few months our little family had joined the rest of the British population (well most of them) and rented a video player, they still cost a fortune back then so unless you had a few bob most people rented them. They were enormous heavy things back then with big piano key controls and no remote control but we thought we were very posh. Now we had one it meant every time there was a children's film on the telly we could tape it to keep my daughter and the other little cousins occupied for a couple of hours. They watched their favourites over and over (and over) again. One of their all-time favourites was Chitty Bang Bang, they watched it so many times it's a wonder the tape didn't wear out and to this day I can still remember every bloody word to every bloody song. They would sit glued to the telly, laughing and singing along until the Child Catcher came on the screen, then my littlest niece would run screaming into the kitchen and cry behind the table until he'd gone again.

As much as she loved Chitty Bang Bang and Mary Poppins my daughter's absolute all-time favourite was Pete's Dragon, a film about a little boy and a giant cartoon dragon called Elliot. She watched it so many times she became obsessed with it, if she stayed over at my parent's house she would take her tape with her so she could still get her fix while she was away from home. One morning she came down to breakfast and demanded two bowls of Weetabix, one for herself and one for her imaginary friend. Now most kids go through the imaginary friend phase when they're little, although most kids don't have a giant invisible dragon as their new friend. I thought he would be called Elliot after the dragon in the film but no, she had named her own personal dragon 'Drag', it must have taken her ages to think that one up.

We just laughed about it at first but after a while Drag became a bit of a pain in the bum, she would insist on an extra place at mealtimes for him, even if we were in a cafe or at someone else's house. If we drove off in the car without waiting for him to get in she would have a fit and go into a panic and woe betide anyone who sat next to us on a bus. She would nudge me and point at the poor person nonstop, getting ever more agitated because someone was sitting on Drag. She would glare at them while whispering to me (loudly) to tell them to move. I would tell her it was ok, Drag quite liked it when somebody sat on his knee but she never believed it. I didn't care what she believed, there was no way I was about to ask a six foot two skinhead if he would mind getting up as he was squashing my daughter's invisible dragon.

My mother thought this new turn of events was really funny and she played along with it all the time, especially in public, she had always liked attracting attention remember. She would walk along with the two of them, singing the songs from the film and talking to the bloody dragon. I would tell her that Drag would never go away if she kept encouraging them but she just laughed. My dad on the other hand wasn't so happy about it. He would happily play along indoors but always insisted that if he was taking my daughter out anywhere she was to leave Drag at home. He hated the thought of people staring at him and pointing while his granddaughter walked along talking to herself like a lunatic.

She was quite cunning for a three-year old, she would agree to leave him behind until they got to wherever they were going. Then she would start prattling away to herself and tell my dad,

"Look who got on a bus and followed me".

Just after her third birthday I decided to get her ears pierced. My parents and my husband were dead against it, they said she was too young, looking back they were right and I regret it now but loads of little girls had them done at that age back then. She was dead brave and thought she was very grown up with her little gold studs. Her experience was nothing like mine had been when, at the age of fifteen I had been mutilated in the back room of a manky shop by an old lady who was equally manky. I took her to a proper salon where everything was clean and sterilised. She couldn't wait until the first six weeks were up and they were properly healed so that we could go and choose some fancier studs.

Every week at a nearby shopping centre a small market would set up a few stalls and one of these sold jewellery. Me and Vicky were looking around one afternoon with the kids and we stopped at the jewellery stall to look at the little ear studs. There were some nice gold sparkly ones that my daughter loved, the lady showed us a few different ones and my daughter took her time deciding which ones to get. She took after me for that, if someone gives us a choice we will be there all day, we are both completely unable to make a decision.

Eventually, after Vicky lost the will to live and said she was going to cry in a minute, my daughter finally made her decision and the lady wrapped the little box of studs up for her. We paid for them and went on our way, Vicky took her baby home and we went to my mother's for a quick cuppa before we went home. On arrival, my daughter showed her Grandma the beautiful new earrings, she was very impressed. In recent years. she had given up preaching about how only prostitutes had pierced ears, mainly because she now had hers done. After I had mine done at age fifteen my mother and Joan next door plucked up the courage to go and get pierced together. I was quite put out after all the years of lecturing I had been forced to listen to, what a hypocrite. She was still insistent that only prostitutes wore ankle strap shoes though, even though every other woman had a pair. Whenever we passed someone wearing a pair I would inwardly cringe, waiting for my mother to open her mouth and get us both beaten up.

At that moment however she was admiring my daughter's new studs.

"Now you've got two pair, haven't you?" she said, "Count with Grandma, one, two."

"Three." said my daughter.

"No pet." said my mother 'one pair in your ears, another in the box, that's one, two, isn't it?"

"Three." said my daughter again. I was getting a bit confused here, she could count up to twenty by now, why was she acting as if she couldn't count?

"How can you have three", I asked her. "One there and one there, that's two."

"Yes." she said "But with this other box that's three, isn't it?"

With that she pulled another little box out of her shirt pocket containing another pair of gold studs. She had helped herself from the stall while none of us were looking. Oh, my god, I had bred a shoplifter.

My mother was mortified, all she could say was,

"Thank God your father's not here, he would die of shame." She wasn't over reacting at all.

She told me to take her back to the market straight away and own up but it was already past the time when the market packed up and left. Instead I gave her a good talking to and told her she must never, never do anything like that again. She promised she wouldn't and said she was sorry. She said she had only done it because she couldn't decide which ones she wanted. I told her if I did that every time I couldn't make a decision I would probably be in prison until her twenty first birthday.

We decided that we would never tell my dad that his granddaughter was a member of the criminal underworld, it would only shatter his illusions and he would never dare take her shopping again. Once again, my mother blamed Frank and Sheila's dodgy genes, there were no criminals on our side of the family she said. I could have told her that was a matter of opinion, I had always found her singing to be criminal. I could have but I didn't, with the discovery of jewellery thief in the family she'd had enough to deal with already that day.

CHAPTER TEN

She's Behind You

Christmas 1983 was now upon us. Every year my daughter seemed to get more and more presents, the Christmas tree could hardly be seen behind the huge pile of presents in front of it. When Christmas morning came around it was the usual story, me and my husband up at the crack of dawn too excited to sleep while upstairs, the three-and a half year old that should have been up with us, ripping off paper was still fast asleep in bed.

She would get so excited the night before that she couldn't get to sleep, when she finally dropped off it would be so late that she would sleep in on the big day. My husband would be beside himself, banging around the house trying to wake her up, while she slept on, dead to the world. Finally, when he could wait no longer he would rush into her room and bellow in her ear,

"WAKE UP, HE'S BEEN!"

This would usually do the trick, then he would drag her down the stairs and shove her at the pile of presents before she had time to get one eye open. He was more of a big kid than she was, I think it was because he always had miserable childhood Christmases with Frank and Sheila, he had never been given anything he ever asked for so he always wanted loads of things for our daughter. We always spent far more on presents than we planned because he never knew when to stop buying things, there was always 'just one more'. He is still the same now, although he doesn't charge into her room these days screaming that Father Christmas has been. I don't think her husband would appreciate that.

On this particular Christmas morning, there was a massive present beside the tree from my parents, it was far too large to fit underneath it. On unwrapping it my daughter almost fainted with joy. My mother had managed to find a three-foot tall, giant stuffed dragon. 'Drag' had come to life, he was no longer a figment of my daughter's imagination. She was overjoyed and began talking to him straight away, I knew there would be one extra at the dinner table this year.

I had a feeling my dad might have had a hand in this, if his granddaughter was towing a massive stuffed toy behind her and talking to that instead of herself, people might not think she was 'special' and judge him for it. Bless him, he was still going to any lengths to avoid attracting attention. Although a three-foot dragon might get him a few looks.

My mother had another reason to be excited this Christmas. This year she was taking my daughter to her very first pantomime and she couldn't wait. She loved going to the Christmas Panto, I had been dragged along every year until finally around about the time I was eleven I had dug my heels in and refused to go any more, it was far too embarrassing, sitting with a load of four and five year olds shouting,

"He's behind you!"

My mother had got me a ticket as well so all three of us were going. My daughter kept asking me what Panto was but how do you explain it to a three-year old. That there's always a boy who's really a girl dressed as a boy, that there will be a couple of strange ladies who are really men in ladies' clothes and wigs and don't get me started on the horse or cow that was really two people bent over holding onto each other inside a costume. It sounded a lot like Frank and Sheila had described their fortnight in Mykonos.

Anyway, the afternoon of the panto arrived and there were the three of us, sitting on the front row of the balcony. We had already had a bit of a performance of our own when my daughter wanted to bring Drag to the show. I had to explain that we didn't have a ticket for him but she wasn't happy about leaving him behind. I was starting to see that things wouldn't be as simple now that her imaginary friend had become real. Eventually she stopped moaning and sat back to watch as the curtains on the stage began to open. As the music started up she looked a bit shell shocked, I had forgotten how loud it was. She soon got used to the noise though and was really enjoying it, just not half as much as my mother was. She was booing and hissing when the baddie came on, shouting out the usual "Oh no you didn't", and singing along loudly with all the songs. I could see how much she had missed the last ten years of this. She had taken my brother once when he was small but he hated it, the music was too loud for him and he had a panic attack every time the audience started shouting. He flatly refused to go any more and no amount of bribing or threatening could make him change his mind.

When it was time for the interval we queued up for ice creams in little tubs and sat back down in our seats to wait for the second half to begin. Once again, my mother threw herself into the whole thing, completely unaware of the nudges and sniggers that the other adults were giving each other every time she started shouting and singing. It was like every wedding we'd ever been to.

As always happened in pantos, around half way through the second half the 'star' of the show would ask if any of the children wanted to come up on stage and help him with his song. Around half the kids would jump up, waving and shouting, hoping to get picked while the other half tried to disappear into their seats, praying to be left alone. I had been one of the second group when I was little (taking after my dad), I would try and make myself as small as possible so that the spotlight wouldn't find me. Meanwhile my mother would be trying to wrestle my arm into the air while shouting,

"Over here, over here!" She was determined that one of us would be 'discovered'.

Luckily, I was never picked so she never got to brag about her child being in show business just as she had been.

As soon as we got to that bit and Buttons or whoever it was started to look for volunteers I knew what was coming next. Sure enough, my mother was asking my daughter if she wanted to go up on the stage and help, while she was asking her she was already trying to prise her from her seat. My daughter looked terrified and said no she didn't want to go, she wanted to stay where she was. My mother wasn't taking no for an answer though, she was telling her how she would enjoy it once she was up there. The spotlight was swinging in our direction and I knew there wasn't much time, I had to rescue my reluctant 'star' from my mother's clutches before she started dangling her over the balcony to get her noticed. Years later I was reminded of that day when I saw Michael Jackson on the news, dangling baby Blanket from his hotel window.

I told my mother to leave her alone, she didn't want to be 'discovered' and that was that. If she kept pushing her she would put her off pantos for life and then she would have nobody to use as an excuse to go herself. Reluctantly she gave up and sat back to watch the other children being ritually humiliated in front of hundreds of people. She could never understand why we didn't want to be the centre of attention like she did, I think it must have been something in her genes. Thank god, we had escaped them.

When the panto was over we left the theatre and got the bus back home again. My mother promised to take us again the following year, that would be something to look forward to.

Not for the first time I wondered why my husband always seemed to have something important to do whenever an outing with Grandma came up.

Back home I spent the next few days trying to find somewhere to put all the toys and games that Father Christmas had delivered to our house. I supposed we could leave some at my mother's house so that my daughter could play with them when she was there. I had been doing this for the last few years, much to my mother's annoyance. Her spare room was full of toys that never got played with. The only thing my daughter ever wanted to play with at my parent's house was my brother's Lego. She loved it and spent hours building houses and cars and god knows what else. Most of the Lego had been mine when I was little, it had been passed on to my brother and then he had added to it over the years until there were boxes and boxes of it.

I mentioned before that my daughter was an animal lover. She also loved any kind of insect, much to my mother's horror (she was and is completely petrified of spiders) and she was always picking them up and bringing them in from the garden. Whenever she built a Lego house she always went outside to find a little tenant to put in it before she put the roof on.

Usually this was one of the hundreds of wood lice that lived in my dad's garden, they were always named Woody (well she was only three). She would sneak off when my mother's back was turned, come back with the biggest 'Woody' she could find, then brick the poor little bugger up alive in its Lego house. She always threw a few leaves in with it for food though I never knew if that's what they ate or not.

That would have been all well and good except for the fact that my brother was also completely terrified of insects, birds, moths, worms, anything that lived in the garden really. He would come home from school to find his niece had been playing with his stuff again and set about putting it all away. The Lego bricks all went in separate compartments in the boxes and he liked to keep it all in order. He would start to dismantle the houses she had built that day, unaware that each little house contained a little surprise. As soon as poor Woody saw a sliver of daylight he would make a break for escape, usually straight into my brother's hands. This would usually result in my brother throwing the Lego as far away from himself as possible while running shrieking for the door. My mother would come to see what all the commotion was about and then join him, heading for the kitchen in case the tenant in question was a spider. My dad said it was highly amusing watching them both trying to get through the doorway at once. There was no motherly instinct at play whenever there might be a spider involved, she would trample her only son to death to get out of the path of a daddy longlegs.

I would usually get a phone call a bit later on telling me to get my daughter under control and to stop her bringing creepy crawlies into the house. It was just one more thing that she didn't get from our side of the family according to my mother, although on this one she was probably right. This one had her father written all over it.

From the time she started walking he would drag her around the garden, lifting up rocks and peering underneath to show her the things that lived there. She would run into the house clutching all sorts of creatures to show me, it's a good job I wasn't like my mother and brother. Once she brought in some frogs in that she couldn't keep hold of and we spent the next hour chasing them around the furniture before taking them back outside. When she got a bit older she kept pet lizards that had to be fed live crickets. This appalled my mother who refused to go anywhere near them, especially when it was their dinner time, she wouldn't even look at the crickets in the bag.

Keeping the lizards was a good little hobby for her for a while although the time she forgot to fasten the bag of crickets back up properly was quite memorable. They all escaped and went all over the house. For the next week or so it was like living in the outback with the sound of them chirruping away all night long, it drove us nuts. Eventually we rounded some up and the rest must have died of starvation because the noise stopped and we were once more able to sleep nights. For the time that they were loose though we had no visits from my mother so it wasn't all bad.

CHAPTER ELEVEN

Hell on Wheels

It seemed like a good idea at the time. Our next door but one neighbours had a rare night off from looking after their four children and asked me and my husband to go for a night out with them. We had never been out with them before but we readily agreed and dropped our offspring at my parent's before heading off for our big night out. We were expecting to go down to the pub or out for something to eat but our neighbours had other plans. Looking back, we should have got to know them a bit better before agreeing to spend the evening with them, then we might not have been so shocked when they took us to their favourite place in all the world, the Roller Disco. Apparently, this was their favourite pastime whenever they could get away and they were quite good at it. I was horrified, I hadn't worn roller skates since I was about eight years old when me and my childhood friend Denise used to share a pair. We took turns wearing them or we wore one each and hobbled up and down the street as if we were in some sort of weird three-legged race. My husband was equally horrified, he hadn't skated since he was a little kid either and then hardly ever as he left that to his sisters while he went out climbing trees and jumping off buildings onto piles of old mattresses (we knew how to live before Play Station).

But we were here now so there was nothing for it but to give it a go. The first obstacle was the skates themselves, they were enormous, big heavy clumpy boots with loads of wheels on them. It took forever to lace them up and then once they were on it was near impossible to lift your feet off the floor, each leg seemed to weigh half a ton. Then there was the roller rink, it wasn't all that big and there were a lot of people on it already, mostly teenagers. It had a wooden floor and the noise was deafening as all the pairs of skates thundered across it, you couldn't even hear the music that was playing so I don't know why it was called a disco. Dancing would be impossible while you were wearing these things on the end of your legs anyway, it would be like trying to strut your stuff while sinking in quicksand.

Our neighbours, Pete and Elaine said we would soon get the hang of it and then they left us to it and skated off together doing some sort of synchronised movements, they made it look quite easy. It wasn't. The pair of us spent the first twenty minutes clinging onto the rail at the edge of the rink or trying to hold each other up. Eventually we got up the nerve to venture out onto the floor properly, taking it very slowly we managed a full lap of the rink without falling over, this wasn't so difficult really once you got into it. We got a bit over confident after that and started to go a bit faster, we had both overlooked the fact that we had no idea how to stop. All was going well until we got separated, I found myself carried along by a big group of skaters behind me, I couldn't get out of their way, I didn't know how to turn, stop or slow down so I did the only thing I could, I went faster. I figured if I could just get around the next turn I could grab onto the barrier and stop myself. Unfortunately, before I managed to do that I felt one of my legs going much faster than the other one, what happened next is still a bit of a blur. I suddenly realised that both of my feet were no longer touching the floor and I went down like a sack of spuds. The twenty or so people that had been inches behind me had no chance to swerve around me and so I took them all out with me. They in turn took out the people that were behind them and so on and so on until there was a giant pyramid of bodies with me at the very bottom, I think for the second time in my life I may have blacked out. Everyone disentangled themselves and got up leaving just me on the floor. The way I had fallen one leg had gone up behind me and one of the wheels on my skate had stuck into the bottom of my back, I realised I couldn't move my legs. Oh, my god, I was paralyzed, I was terrified, one stupid visit to a Roller Disco and now I would be in a wheelchair for ever. Now my daughter was out of her buggy she would be pushing me around instead, how would we manage? (I wasn't being at all over dramatic).

Before I had a chance to plan my life as a disabled person I was rudely removed from the floor by a pair of overzealous first aiders. They each grabbed me by an armpit and dragged me across the rink, past the crowd of disgruntled skaters to the small refreshment area where they manhandled me into a plastic chair. I wasn't sure that's how you were supposed to treat a person who had just broken their back but they wouldn't listen to my protests. They said they had seen it all before and my legs would soon come back, they spoke as if my legs had just popped out for a minute. I was about to tell them how I was going to sue them for making things worse and adding to my injuries when I realised they were right, I could feel my legs again, I also felt really stupid.

By this time my other half had managed to stagger across to check on me, he said he was glad I was ok, he had been worried for a minute. Then he said it was also one of the funniest things he had ever seen, I had gone out like a dying swan. One of the first aiders said it was the biggest pile up they had ever had there, I had broken some kind of record. Pete and Elaine came over as well and said the best thing was to throw myself straight back into it, I would have liked to throw myself straight at the two of them. Why would two grown up adult people want to come here and skate round and round with a load of kids. Still, there was another hour left until we were going home so I hauled myself out of my chair and headed back out onto the floor. This time I went really slowly and stayed near the barrier, I had learned my lesson, I wasn't going to get cocky again. My husband was tottering along behind me (I thought), when a voice boomed out of the speakers telling all novices to clear the floor immediately as it was time for the speed skating. I grabbed the barrier and pulled myself to the exit, once out of the rink I turned to talk to my husband, only to find he wasn't behind me at all. Just as I started to scan the room for him the lights suddenly went out, it was almost pitch black now. The music was turned up full blast and suddenly ultra violet strobe lights started flashing everywhere, I was hoping he had found somewhere to prop himself up or these lights would make him so dizzy he'd fall over. All I could see were figures speeding round and round the rink, the lights flashing so fast now everything was just flickering. After a few minutes I became aware of people laughing, some of them were pointing. I tried to see what they were pointing at but it was too hard to see with all the lights flashing. Eventually my eyes became accustomed to the lights and I could make out a figure on the other side of the rink. This figure was clinging to the wall like some kind of Spiderman impersonator, arms and legs spread-eagled like a starfish. I began to giggle along with everyone else, thank god, I had made it off the floor in time, that could have been me up there making a spectacle of myself. I'd already provided enough entertainment for one night.

Then as the lights changed and became slower I suddenly realised that the jacket this poor fool was wearing looked familiar. Oh no, that's why my husband hadn't been behind me, he had got stuck on the other side when the speed skaters came on and now he was clinging onto the wall for dear life. It seemed like ages before everything slowed down again and I could go and rescue him. He wasn't amused at all. We dragged each other across to the little cafe and sat there until we could catch the eye of Pete and Elaine. Every time we spotted them they just smiled and waved at us, they were having a ball, complete unaware that we were in hell.

After they had whizzed past us another fifty times I finally managed to signal to them that we had had enough, we were going home with or without them. They said they would come with us and we all left together. The pair of us were in a right state, limping and hobbling to the bus stop while they bounded along like a couple of kids, and they were about ten years older than us. They asked if we'd enjoyed it and would we like to go again.

Were they mad? There was no way in hell I would ever go back and try that again, we were a couple of nervous wrecks and my back was killing me. We politely declined and told them it wasn't really for us. If they ever fancied a trip to the cinema or a few drinks down the pub we would be right there with them. Otherwise please leave us the hell alone.

For the next few days I spent most of my time standing up, it hurt too much to sit down. The bottom of my back and my bum was absolutely black and blue and I walked strangely for a fortnight. Since that time my husband has had super-fast motorcycles, jet skis, quad bikes and god knows what else but nothing on earth would ever make him put on another pair of roller skates. To this day, he has a funny turn whenever he sees strobe lights. People think he's epileptic when he develops a twitch until I tell them he's just reliving a traumatic experience.

Incidentally, at the age of forty-nine I took up ice skating (must have been a hormone thing) and managed to learn a few moves and spins. I collected quite a lot of bruises along the way as well as a fractured wrist and my elbows are now a completely different shape but at least I never caused as much of an uproar in four years on the ice as I did in that one night at the Roller Disco.

CHAPTER TWELVE

School Daze

Now that my daughter was four and a half it was time for her to start nursery school. The nursery was a small building in the same school that she would be attending when she turned five. The first morning she had to go I was expecting tears and tantrums, after all she had never really been away from me except for the time she spent with her grandparents. I was dreading it really but the teachers had said that the mums could stay for a bit to get the little ones settled before we left them so that was something.

My mother wasn't happy about it, she didn't agree with nursery school, she said there would be time enough for all that when she was five. I didn't want her to go really either but I thought it would do her good to mix with other kids and it would make the transition to school easier as she would be going with the rest of the children from the nursery class.

We arrived just before nine o clock and I showed her where to hang her coat up and change into her sandshoes. To my amazement she changed her shoes, waved me goodbye and told me to go home now, she would see me at lunchtime. I couldn't believe it, all around me other mothers were trying to disentangle themselves from screaming, crying children refusing to let go of them and go into class. Meanwhile there was mine, skipping off to play without so much as a backwards glance at me, I didn't know whether to be proud or insulted.

When lunchtime came, I went back to pick her up, she came out with armfuls of paintings and drawings and said she'd had a great time and she was going back tomorrow, I couldn't get over how easy it had been, I had been dreading it for nothing.

She settled in really well and made lots of little friends, she also fell in love with her teacher, she told me she looked like a Princess and called her 'Beautiful Miss Dobbs'. She was quite pretty really especially when you saw her together with the other teacher, I can't remember her name but I will never forget her legs. They were like tree trunks and she wore the same 'American Tan' tights that I had wanted all those years ago. Unfortunately, she had never been introduced to the art of shaving her legs and therefore had quite a growth going on underneath them. There was so much dark hair matted against the nylon her legs looked patterned, also some of the longer hairs would poke through her tights as if they were trying to escape from the rest of the jungle. It was both revolting and fascinating at the same time and it was really hard to keep eye contact with her when she spoke, no matter how hard I tried my eyeballs were compelled to keep looking down at her legs. From the waist down she looked like a gorilla in ladies clothing, at least they would keep her warm in winter.

Those six months flew by and before we knew it, suddenly the day had come for my daughter to start 'rea' school. I wasn't worried this time as she was used to going to nursery every day and she would be moving up with a class full of her friends, this should be a doddle.

I shouldn't have been so confident. From the minute her new teacher set foot in the playground to collect the new class my daughter took an instant dislike to her. She was called Mrs Turner and she wasn't what you would call the maternal type. She took one look at my daughter clinging to my legs and told me just to leave her and go home, she would be fine once I'd gone. I tried to do as she said but it was hard, every time I looked back I could see Mrs Turner trying to rugby tackle my daughter into the classroom and I could still hear the screaming as I left the playground. I felt awful and cried all the way home. I consoled myself with the thought that the teacher was probably right, she would have settled in with her friends once I'd been gone ten minutes. When I picked her up for lunch she would be fine.

She wasn't. When she came out of class it was with a big red face and puffy eyes. She informed me that she hated it and she was never going back.

So began a few weeks of screaming and crying every morning, I would leave her at the classroom door every day and then have to pass the classroom window on my way out. For the first few days she would be pounding on the glass with her little fists begging me to come back, after that, whenever I looked in I would see Mrs Turner practically sitting on her to keep her away from the window. It was absolutely heart-breaking and I hated it. I began to get an inkling of what my mother had gone through with my little brother when he wouldn't go to school, although I wasn't yet at the stage of dragging her there by her legs.

After a fortnight of this I couldn't take any more, it was too awful, even the kids that had been a bit weepy at first had settled down now. I had made up my mind, that was it I would take her out of school and teach her myself at home, how hard could it be? She was already reading.

I was so busy making plans in my head I didn't realise at first that she wasn't crying, she went in with the other kids and I turned around to go home. I passed the window and looked in, expecting to see the usual wrestling match going on between her and Mrs Turner. Instead she was sitting at her desk getting her crayons out, she looked up, waved to me and stuck her tongue out. Just like that it was over, we had cracked it, what a relief.

After that we never looked back, she took to school like a duck to water. Every morning she trotted off in with the other kids, barely pausing long enough to say goodbye, and when I picked her up again she would be all smiles, shoving whatever creation she had made that day under my nose.

As those first months went by she got very involved in everything that was going on, she paraded around the hall in an Easter bonnet, sang her heart out at the Harvest Festival, and got her first taste of fame in the school Christmas play. She was so excited when she was given her role, it was perfect for her. Around a dozen kids were joined together, making up the body of a giant dragon (why there was a dragon in the Christmas play escapes me now).

She was so proud to be on the very end of the line, playing the dragon's bum. She even got to wiggle it.

The only time she cried again was at the school sports day. She was in the running race with half the rest of the class, they had to run a couple of hundred yards and first to cross the tape won a prize. She was running full pelt, leaving all the other kids behind her. My mother tried to take a photo but she was going so fast all that appeared on the photo was the toe of her sandshoe. Just as she was about to cross the line she stopped dead and burst into tears. I ran onto the field to see what was the matter with her,

"What's wrong, why did you stop?" I asked her.

She pointed at the piece of tape that was strung up for her to run through and, still sobbing, said,

"I can't jump over that, it's too high."

Bless her, she thought after all that running, every kid in the class had to jump over a two-foot hurdle. She never did get her prize.

At first, we thought she was going to take after her dad, at school he had been very sporty, getting medals for gymnastics, swimming, running and god knows what else. He could jump higher than anyone else and was a whizz on the trampoline. P.E was about the only thing he ever turned up for though, that and school dinners. In High School, he had been so fond of school dinners he would finish whatever was on the menu that day and then go to the other High School up the road for another one. In those days, there was no security in schools like there is today and anyone could wander in and out. He would tell me if I had been forced to eat Sheila's cooking growing up I would have done the same, there was no cigarette ash in school dinners. He was at the other school so often he joined the woodwork class without anyone realising he didn't actually go to that school. His woodwork project ended up on display in the school as it was so good but still nobody twigged. He actually got on better at the school he didn't really go to than the one he was actually supposed to attend.

Anyway, it soon became apparent that our daughter had inherited her mother's sporting prowess, not her father's. Her gymnastic skills were about as good as mine, I could never do handstands with the other girls as being upside down gave me vertigo, also I wasn't crazy about flashing my big, baggy navy blue knickers to all and sundry. Her dad couldn't understand how someone with half of his genes couldn't do back flips at will, he would spend hours showing her how to walk on her hands but to no avail. She was happier on her own two feet.

Mind you, walking on his hands has always been his party piece, especially after a beer or two. Every little kid in our family has been given a demonstration at some time or other (even if they didn't want one), as well as friend's kids, neighbours, visitors or whoever happened to be around at the time. Today he has arthritis in both wrists which he blames on years of plastering, I blame it on years of acting the fool, walking miles up and down various gardens on his hands. With a talent like that it's a wonder Frank and Sheila didn't sell him to the circus as a kid.

It also soon became apparent that my daughter had inherited my early clumsiness, when I had been her age I could fall over fresh air and it seemed like every other day I had a split lip or smashed nose. She was fine on her own two feet but stick her on anything with wheels and you could bet your last pound that within ten minutes we would be wiping up snot and blood. I became accustomed to this quite quickly but the same couldn't be said for my mother who would run around flapping like a headless chicken. She would immediately drag out her medical kit even though it contained nothing but a reel of Elastoplast and a stick to stop the bleeding if you cut yourself shaving.

Usually the first thing she did was run to the cupboard and grab the butter, then she would proceed to slather whatever the affected area happened to be in great globs of Lurpak. It was her answer to everything,

Bump on the head? Slap on some butter.

Burnt finger? Stick it in butter.

Grazed knee? Butter again. If she happened to be on a diet she would use margarine which had the same effect, which was none at all. She wasn't alone on this one though, growing up, all my friends' mothers did the same thing so at any one time there were always a few of us sporting yellow grease on various bits of our bodies.

My mother had some strange remedies for when you were ill, her favourite one being butter and treacle mixed together (she had a real thing about butter). She would give us this for various ailments although I don't recall ever feeling better for it. If we had a sore throat she would give us it to soothe the soreness, if we felt sick she would shovel it down us to make us vomit. If we had a belly ache she would say it would coat our stomachs although how it could coat your stomach while at the same time making you vomit always escaped me.

She also had some strange ideas about taking pills, to this day she still tells people this one.

If you swallow pills with a drink of milk it stops the pills from working. You can take them with water, tea, coffee, fruit juice, anything but milk. There is something in the milk that renders any pill or tablet completely useless. She will not be wrong on this no matter how much you argue with her. I once asked her what would happen if someone wanting to commit suicide swallowed two bottles of sleeping pills with a glass of milk.

"Nothing." she said. She told me they would have absolutely no effect on the person at all. I asked her where she had got this information from but she just said it was common knowledge. Maybe it was but not to anyone I ever met.

Despite being clumsy at least our daughter was better at swimming than I had been so some of that must have come from her dad's side. She learnt to swim when she was about six and was really at home in the water. I could manage a length of breaststroke and that was me finished. I hated swimming lessons at school, the only thing I remember about them is splashing around, clinging desperately to a polystyrene brick while a butch woman in a tracksuit walked along the edge of the pool poking me with a long stick.

One day when we were all at the swimming baths my husband gave us a lesson on swimming underwater, he could dive under the water and swim to the other end of the baths before popping up. We didn't get quite that far but we both thought we had done really well, we had both taken deep breaths, dived under and swam quite a little distance before resurfacing. When we did everyone in the pool was having a good laugh at our expense, apparently while we both thought we were swimming somewhere near the bottom of the pool we were actually only about a foot under the water and worse still we had been swimming along with just our bums sticking out of the water.

We tried again a few more times but it was no good, our bums just refused to go under, it was as if we both had built in floatation devices. Once again, my husband despaired of us, he couldn't get his head around why we found it so hard when it came so naturally to him.

I would tell my daughter it didn't matter, we couldn't all be good at everything and besides, we were both better at spelling than he was (and she was only just six by then). As a kid, he had been dyslexic although in those days you were just called 'thick' and put in the 'special' class along with the kids that couldn't tie their own shoelaces and ate their own bogies. As a result of this he has never been able to spell properly. I could fill a book just with some examples of the notes I have been left by him over the years. One of my particular favourites was waiting for me one afternoon when I came in, he had a few air rifles in those days and used to go off into the fields near us for target practice. On this day, he had gone off with his gun but not before scribbling off this little ditty:

Back soon
Gone shouting at the paddok
X

I knew what he meant but all afternoon I kept sniggering to myself at the thought of him, all by himself, standing in the middle of a field screaming at the top of his voice.

CHAPTER THIRTEEN

Day Trippers

That first year of primary school flew by and before we knew it summer had come around again and it was time for the annual school trip. The teachers at this school obviously had no imagination as every year for god knows how long they took the kids to the same place. They always started off with a visit to the Rock Factory (this was a place where they made actual sticks of rock, not a nightclub), and then on to a park near the seaside where there were lots of animals. To top everything off they would all get on a little train that dropped everyone off at the beach where they would spend the last hour and eat their sandwiches. Every year they would try and rope some of the mothers in to go along and help and this particular year it was my turn. I would be given a little group of children to keep an eye on for a few hours, how hard could it be? I had no idea what I was letting myself in for.

My mother tried to get in on the act and said she would come along and help. I squashed that idea flat straight away, I would have enough to cope with already without having to worry about my mother insulting the other women and trying to slap other people's children. Not to mention the commotion she would cause on the coach with her singing and announcing the names of every village we passed through. I told her thankyou but there were enough volunteers already.

The morning of the trip arrived and we all met up at the school. There were three or four teachers, a few other mothers, thirty-six hyperactive children and me. We volunteer stood in a line to be 'given' our children for the day, I had five in my little group, consisting of my own child, three others and Terry. I should have realised something was up when the other mothers all let out a collective sigh of relief on hearing that Terry was in my group. Terry was what you would call 'a bit of a handful' although at this stage I was still completely unaware of this. My second clue should have been the sight of Terry's mother who had come to wave him off. In hindsight, I think she just wanted to make absolutely sure that he had really gone. She was practically dancing in the car park and couldn't stop laughing, before the bus driver even started the engine she was already legging it down the road, I think she may have been skipping.

It started off well enough. For the first half hour, the kids entertained themselves by looking in each other's lunch boxes and swapping the stuff they didn't want for things they liked. That sorted they started eating the mountains of sweets that they had smuggled on to the bus, it was a bit early for sweets, being only just gone nine o clock but it kept them all quiet for a while, while their mouths were full of junk they couldn't talk as much. Half an hour later the first case of travel sickness kicked in, one little girl at the back began heaving half a family sized bag of Opal Fruits into her lap. This seemed to set off some kind of chain reaction and soon half the bus was vomiting into plastic carrier bags, lunchboxes, hats and whatever other vessels the poor teachers could find. For once, my daughter wasn't throwing up, this was quite unusual as she had inherited my childhood travel sickness and usually spent most journeys with her head in a bucket. She was sitting quite happily with her best friend, Beautiful Elizabeth, since she had left Miss Dobbs behind at nursery school she had met Elizabeth and decided she was beautiful enough to take on the title. Out of the five kids in my group two of them were being sick, including Terry, I felt bad for him, he looked so pale and sorry for himself. I was still not seeing the 'real' Terry, that would happen sometime later.

The smell that began to fill the bus was horrendous, so bad that even some of the kids not affected by travel sickness began retching as well, I'm sure the bus driver was also gagging as he drove along, his shoulders were definitely heaving. We opened every window we could and tried not to breathe until we reached our first destination.

Luckily, the Rock Factory wasn't too far away from home and soon we were ferrying the vomit scented little darlings across the car park and into the first stop on the factory tour, the room where all the rock was being cooked and stirred in big cauldrons. Everything smelt sickly sweet, not exactly the thing to settle thirty-six little stomachs but they all seemed to recover quickly and by the time we got to the last bit where the finished products were for sale they were queuing up to spend their pocket money on sticks of rock and bags of hard sweets. No doubt that lot would be making an appearance again on the way home, I collected as many plastic bags as I could, just in case.

When we came out the kids were allowed to play for half an hour before we got back on the bus, there was a small park with swings and slides and stuff so they all made a bee line for that. There was also a small stream with a tiny little bridge over it, this was like a magnet to my mini David Attenborough, who grabbed Beautiful Elizabeth and set off to look for frogs. I followed them and warned them to keep away from the stream, if anyone got wet I had no spare clothes with me. They both promised to be careful. I looked over to the playground where I could see Terry hanging upside down from the climbing frame, he seemed a lot better now. I only looked away for a couple of seconds but that was long enough, I heard a splash, then, "Whoops" and turned back round to see my daughter up to her ankles in the stream.

"Sorry" she said, "I slipped".

She was wearing plastic jellybean sandals so that was ok but her socks were drenched. Luckily one of the teachers had brought some spare socks (she had obviously been here before) so she put a pair on and then spent the rest of the day complaining that they were too tight. I told her she should have listened and been a bit more careful, I really should have learned my lesson by now and just dressed her in wellies all the time.

We all got back on the bus again, the driver had left all the doors and windows open for the last hour so the smell had diminished quite a bit by then. Not too long after that we arrived at the park, now the fun would really begin. I gathered my five little charges and we headed off to look at all the animals. After each stop I did a quick head count before we moved on to the next cage or enclosure, Terry was becoming more excitable by the minute and kept trying to sneak off to join his friend in a different group. I told him to stay put in case he got lost, what would his mother say if we went home without him? Secretly I thought she would probably be delighted.

Halfway round the park two of the girls decided they needed a wee so we had to find the toilets. They wouldn't go in on their own so I had to leave Terry and another little boy in the doorway for a minute, I made Terry promise not to move an inch and told him I could still see him. Each time I looked up the two of them were still there. Suddenly there was a commotion because one of the girls didn't have enough toilet roll and by the time I found her another roll and turned around again Terry was gone. The other little boy was still there but standing by himself. I ran over to him.

"Where's Terry"? I gasped.

"Over there Miss" he said and pointed towards one of the enclosures that contained some goats. Sure enough there was Terry, legging it over the fence into the pen. I grabbed the other four kids and ran towards him, the two little girls that had been to the toilet were running along with us still trying to pull up their knickers, I had rudely interrupted them and yanked them out of the cubicles half dressed.

I caught up to Terry just as he made it over the fence and grabbed him by the collar.

"Get out of there, what do you think you're doing?" I yelled.

"Nothing" he said, "I just wanted to ride them."

I was halfway through telling him that you didn't ride goats, that they didn't like that, when my daughter piped up.

"You can ride them, I used to ride Billy."

There then followed a discussion on Billy. Where was he now, did I have any pictures of him, was he in a zoo like this one? I shut them all up by promising them a ride on a donkey if we came across any when we got to the beach. I did another head count and we set off again to see the other attractions. When we got to the part where all the birds were kept I realised I only had four heads, Terry had given me the slip again. This time I couldn't see him anywhere, I started to panic, how would I explain the fact that I had lost a six-year old. We started going around the other little groups to see if he had joined any of them but there was no sign of him. Just when I thought I might faint with fear, I saw one of the teachers walking towards me holding Terry by the neck.

"Does this one belong to you?" she asked cheerfully "I just found him halfway up that tree over there, he said he was playing hide and seek with you."

I managed to stutter an apology, I only looked away for a second, and it wouldn't happen again, blah, blah. The teacher just laughed.

"Don't worry about it, we're all used to Terry by now, aren't we Terry?" (squeezing his neck a bit harder).

She handed him over and we set off again, this time I stayed a foot behind him, I wasn't going to lose him again. Every two minutes I counted heads, one, two, three, four, five. Terry kept whining that he wanted to walk by himself but I wouldn't let him.

When we had seen just about everything there was to see we started to head towards the meeting place where we were all going to get on the little train, I counted heads again, one, two, three, four, five, six. Dear god I had an extra one, there was another little boy with us. Where had he come from? I asked him his name and which group he had been with, he said he had been with Miss Baker's group. I asked my daughter which teacher was Miss Baker. She said she didn't know any teachers called that and the other kids all agreed with her, there was no Miss Baker at their school. This was getting worse by the minute; this kid wasn't even from our school.

I asked him if he recognised anyone around us but he said no, he couldn't see anyone he knew. When I asked him for the name of his school things got a bit worse, he wasn't even from the same town as us. There was nothing for it but to take him with me and see if the teachers could find out who he belonged to. He didn't seem to be all that bothered that he was lost and was sharing sweets with the other boys. Just as we were in sight of the meeting place I heard someone screeching, I looked round to see a woman running towards us in a blind panic. It turned out to be the woman in charge of the little boy's group, she had lost him half an hour ago and was terrified that he'd been kidnapped. Apparently, this little boy was the other school's Terry, he had been trying to give his group the slip all day. This lady was just like me, one of the mother's that had been lumbered with the naughty kid, I commiserated with her and gave her back her missing person. She looked as stressed as I felt.

By this time all the other groups had turned up and it was time to board the little train to the beach, it was just the same as the train that had carried me and my family to our holiday chalet at Butlins all those years ago. The kids loved it but we weren't on it that long before we arrived at the beach. The kids all began mingling together and getting out their lunch boxes for their picnic, when they'd finished eating they had an hour to play before we set off for home again.

I was still keeping an eye on the five that I was responsible for but it wasn't easy, they all wanted to be off doing something different. Eventually I rounded them all up and took them to the water's edge to paddle. They all took off their shoes and socks and spent ten minutes running in and out of the waves, screaming at the cold water. After a while I got them all out again and they all sat down to dry their feet and put their shoes and socks back on. That was when I realised Terry had done a runner again, that boy was starting to get on my last nerve by now. I started to look around shouting his name and asking the other kids if they had seen him.

"He's there Miss" said one little girl, pointing up the beach.

"Where?" I asked her, I couldn't see him.

"Up there." she said, pointing again.

Then I saw him, halfway up a cliff, (admittedly not a massive cliff but still a cliff). When I shouted at him he even had the nerve to give me a wave. That was the last straw, I'd had enough now, I thought about just sitting down on the sand and crying but luckily one of the teachers came to my rescue. She manhandled Terry down from his perch and told me she would take charge of him now, she told him when we got back she would be having words with his mother. Somehow, I didn't think that would do much good but so long as he was out of my hair I didn't care. Soon we were all back on the bus again, Terry was forced to sit up front with the teacher who kept an eagle eye on him so finally I could relax a bit. As we left the coach park everyone started to sing 'The Wheels on The Bus', my mother would have loved this. Fortunately, after about the fourth time of singing it the first case of travel sickness made an appearance. Then, a few more joined in and soon a fair bit of the picnic food was seeing the light of day again. Once again, everyone was running around trying to find bags and buckets to catch it all. By the time we rolled up back at the school the poor bus driver practically threw us all off, all the other mothers were there waiting for their little darlings, even Terry's. She wasn't best pleased when the teacher took her off for a quiet word though but Terry wasn't at all bothered. He even gave me a big wave as he was dragged off towards home.

I was completely exhausted, physically and mentally drained. It had only been a few hours but I felt like I'd aged ten years in that time. How the teachers coped with that every day was beyond me, I would have gone home sobbing every night. I began to see now why some of them looked so rough and wrinkled, I had always thought Mrs Turner was about sixty, she was probably only thirty-two.

I knew I would have to do it all again next year though. After seeing how mental it all was and how easy it was to lose little kids there was no way I could let mine go off on her own without me. God knows where she might end up. Maybe next year they would take us somewhere different and nicer.

They didn't.

CHAPTER FOURTEEN

Making a Boob

Over the years since my childhood my dad had kept up with his D.I.Y skills, sadly they hadn't improved any. He still went in for outrageous wallpaper in gaudy colours but now he had added a little extra twist, he papered over the doors as well. Admittedly he left a border of a couple of inches all the way round to stop them disappearing into the walls but it was still a sight to behold. It could be very claustrophobic at times and some visitors seemed to have slight panic attacks when they tried to leave.

I used to tell him that this wasn't normal behaviour, other people didn't wallpaper over their doors but it didn't faze him. He said it would soon catch on and then everyone would be doing it. To my knowledge, it never did.

He was still doing his old trick of putting in pieces from different rolls if he ran out of paper, he still thought no one would notice. One year when my daughter was a baby we went away for a few days. My parents had the keys to my house and before we came back they decided to surprise us by buying us a new carpet. My dad fitted it himself so that it would be all ready when we came home, unfortunately he had done his usual trick of measuring the room wrong so the carpet came up about two foot short at one end. Undeterred he carried on and then simply inserted a completely different piece of carpet from some offcuts he had in the shed into the gap. It was a different colour and pattern but he said as it was in the alcove nobody would notice and anyway, we could just stick a table over it.

He had also been doing quite a bit of woodwork for the last few years, he had built my daughter a massive slide with a playhouse built in underneath it. He had seen it in a woodwork magazine and followed the instructions to the letter, it actually turned out really well and lasted for years. He was a dab hand at customising things as well and you could guarantee that some of his inventions were definitely a one off. One example of his handiwork was the dog kennel he had built for the various dogs that came and went over the years. It had actually started life as a fruit machine and it had belonged to me and my husband. I can't remember where it came from but when we were first married we kept it in the big cupboard in our hallway and played on it until we got fed up of it. We took it to my parent's house so my little brother could play on it but the next time we saw it the dog was peering out from underneath the bit where the coins came out when you'd won. My dad had painted the whole thing black but it still looked like a fruit machine, the poor dog looked completely bewildered, no doubt wondering why it had been kicked out of a nice warm house and was now being forced to live in an amusement arcade.

Then came the year he built the love seat in the back garden. He bought it in flat pack form so all he had to do was put it together. Somehow, somewhere along the way he misread the instructions and built it so that instead of the two seats facing each other as they should do on a love seat they actually faced in opposite directions. When he and my mother tried it out they ended up sitting back to back without even being able to see each other. Although this time I thought maybe he had done it on purpose.

Throughout all his D.I.Y disasters my mother was still behind him, constantly egging him on. Whatever mess he made or whatever hideous decorating schemes he came up with she thought it was all marvellous. She would always brag to people about how handy her husband was around the house, how he could turn his hand to anything. I don't know which of them was the most deluded.

Mind you, my mother was a lot more cheerful these days, she was having another crack at the fame game. She and my dad were still going to the same social club that they had joined years ago when I had been forced to babysit but by this time they had somehow wangled themselves onto the committee. There had recently been a vacancy for a bingo caller and, ever eager to get a microphone in her hand, my mother had offered (forced) her services.

Twice a week now she took to the stage and putting on her poshest voice spent the evening calling out 'Two Fat Ladies' and 'Clickety Click, Number Six'. She offered to do a few songs during the interval but nobody seemed to want to take her up on her offer. She was in her element now she was up there in the limelight, she always put on her poshest frocks and added a few sparkling accessories. She looked completely out of place among all the headscarves and anoraks but she didn't care, she was on a stage and people were looking at her, that's all that mattered.

A few years after that my dad was made chairman of the committee and my mother's self-importance knew no bounds. You would have thought she was the Lady Mayoress and she took every opportunity to drop it into a conversation no matter how inappropriate. She would burst in on other people's conversations, always looking for a chance to let everyone know about her important husband and their glamorous life on the social club committee. Behind her back everyone took the mickey out of her but, as usual she was completely oblivious to it all.

Of all the people laughing and poking fun at my mother, none laughed louder than Frank and Sheila. They thought this latest development was hilarious and made unkind jokes and comments all the time. I had to bite my tongue because nobody was worse than those two for exaggerating things to make themselves look more important. It was a clear case of pot and kettle.

Sheila had recently left us all completely gobsmacked by going off and getting a boob job. In the early eighties, nobody we knew had ever heard of normal (I use this term loosely) everyday women getting boob jobs, that was for the rich and famous. Still, Sheila had had enough of people like my mother sniggering at her two fried eggs and so out came the credit cards and off she went to a private clinic. When she came back she looked very different and after a week or so recuperating she couldn't wait to show off the twins. It was so embarrassing, she would whip them out every five minutes showing them to everyone, even if they really would have preferred not to look.

When she showed my husband, he was mortified and didn't know where to put himself. He told her it wasn't right to show your boobs to your only son but she just said it was all the fault of him and his sisters that she had ended up with two fried eggs anyway, they had ruined her bosom. He wasn't impressed by her mothering instinct and apologised for having to be fed when he was a baby. I couldn't imagine her as the nurturing type but he said it was only because she was too cheap to buy formula.

My mother was appalled when she heard about the new boobs and said that Frank and Sheila must have more money than sense. I told her they had been bought on credit and wouldn't really belong to Sheila for another five years. She was even more appalled then, she thought credit card was a dirty word, she wanted to know what was wrong with saving up, why did people get into debt? She had a very short memory.

As soon as the stitches healed and the swelling went down Sheila was off buying new bras and bikinis, soon after that the plastic came out again (the credit cards not the boobs) and several more holidays were booked. She couldn't wait to go topless on the beach with her new look. Before she went she did one more thing to embarrass her poor children, she had a topless photograph done of herself. Now by this time she was fifty-two but could easily pass for a pensioner, the last few years of frazzling in the Spanish sun had not done her wrinkles much good at all. The tight frizzy granny perm also made her look as if she was ready for her bus pass but not to be put off she got into her best Page 3 pose and got in front of the camera.

The result was excruciating, none of us wanted to look at it and when we were forced to look we were lost for words. Frank and Sheila thought it was very sophisticated and had one photo enlarged to hang on the wall. This would have been all very well if they had hung it in their bedroom for their own private amusement but no, they wanted everyone to see how glamorous Sheila was. Therefore, they hung it over the fireplace in the living room where everyone that came into the house would see it. It was hideous, it looked like someone had photo shopped a little old lady's head onto the body of a porn star (a retired one). As soon as you entered the room it would smack you in the face (figuratively speaking) and I used to feel very sorry for the insurance man when he came round every week to collect their premiums. I suppose it wasn't all bad though, at least she had put her teeth in for the photo.

While Sheila was trying to recapture her youth by purchasing a pair of giant knockers, Frank was trying to hang onto his by refusing point blank to go bald. This was no easy thing considering three quarters of his hair had already departed, never to make an appearance again. The bit that he had left was turned into a giant comb over, it was a real feat of engineering, the hair on the top of his head being about a foot long. He somehow wound it around his head and fixed it into place with hairgrips and extra strong hairspray. Every week he went through the biggest can I had ever seen, it was ginormous, I'm sure Frank had quite a bit to do with hole in the ozone layer.

Not content with masking his baldness he also refused to go grey. In his youth, he had black hair so now at the age of fifty-four he dyed it jet black every week. At first, he was satisfied with this but one day while checking the back of his head in the mirror he noticed that his bald bits at the back were made more noticeable by the black hair. Instead of laying off the dye and growing old gracefully he took to the shopping channels on the telly and came up with several cans of black, spray on hair. I'm sure he was being taken advantage of and was actually being sold shoe polish but he was pleased with the results. Despite the name there wasn't actually any hair involved in the spray, whatever it was it just coloured his scalp black. This meant that all around the house he left big black head prints. His pillowcases looked like he had been using them to carry coal around and if he leant back in the armchair he had to have a cover behind his head. Also, he never left the house without a brolly, even in summer as one quick shower was enough to turn him into Alice Cooper. It was hilarious but nevertheless, with his hair and her boobs they thought they looked like a glamorous, celebrity couple.

I had always thought that my parents were the strangest people I knew but I was starting to have second thoughts. I suppose both sets of parents were strange in their own particular way, there wasn't really that much to choose between.

CHAPTER FIFTEEN

Driving Miss Dozy

When my daughter was about seven I decided I'd had enough of travelling by bus or being the passenger in our car so I decided it was finally time for me to learn to drive. Driving was another thing that had always come naturally to my husband, he had taught himself to drive when he was fourteen and by the time he was sixteen he was going to school every day in his own car, even though he was under age and completely illegal. Therefore, he saw no need to waste money on driving lessons for me, he would teach me himself, simple. With our track record, we should have known what a bad idea that was.

The day of the first lesson came around and we got into the car with our daughter in the back. He drove us off into the country where it was quiet and I got into the driving seat. His first words as I took to the wheel were hardly confidence inspiring.

"Remember one thing" he told me.
"What's that?"

"This isn't a car, it's a lethal weapon. Actually, it's a killing machine, one wrong move and someone ends up dead."

I didn't think you got this pep talk with the regular driving schools. As you can imagine I was already a nervous wreck before I started the engine. This set the tone for the rest of the lesson really, things went from bad to worse. Instead of gently instructing me he would bellow instructions in my ear, punctuated by lots of banging on the dashboard. I was far too terrified to listen now that I knew I was actually in charge of a lethal weapon and not a Datsun Sunny, so nothing he screamed at me was getting through.

By the end of the lesson I was traumatised and our daughter was lying on the floor in the back of the car assuming the crash position (there were no rear seat belts back then). I never wanted to get into a car with my husband ever again but by now he was on a mission, he was going to teach me to drive if it killed him. I thought it would probably kill all of us.

After that, Sunday afternoons become a nightmare. We would finish our dinner and then it was time to go off for another lesson. My daughter would beg to be let off, sometimes we would drop her off at my parent's house but most times she was forced to come along with us, assuming the position in the back as soon as I took to the wheel. Every week it ended the same, lots of screaming and shouting, tears and tantrums, and that was just my husband. He would get me so wound up that I was incapable of remembering which pedal was which, what gear I was in or what bit of the road I should be on. The big finale was always the moment when I jumped out of the car, screaming that I would walk home, just leave me alone. Then running, shrieking after the car when he did just that.

Eventually, after a few more weeks of this we decided that this 'teach your wife to drive' thing maybe wasn't the best idea for all of us. We were practically on the edge of a divorce and my daughter had developed a phobia of cars. It was decided that I would take a few weeks off driving to try and de-traumatise myself and then I would book some lessons with a proper driving instructor who wouldn't threaten to strangle me with my own seatbelt every time I tried to go the wrong way on a roundabout.

And so it began. A long line of driving instructors, each one worse than the one before. I had always had a knack of finding strange people, I mean look what I was born into but now I really seemed to be outdoing myself. The first instructor that turned up was a middle-aged man, he seemed quite nice and was very patient, I told myself I was in good hands here. About half an hour into my first lesson I noticed he was looking at my feet quite a lot. I put this down to him wanting to make sure I was using the right pedals. A little later on he made a comment about liking the colour of the varnish on my toes. A little strange I thought but maybe he was just trying to put me at ease. I didn't think that much of it. I got through the lesson and he told me I had done very well. I wasn't crying as I usually was by this time so I had to agree with him. I arranged another lesson for the next week and went off, quite pleased with myself.

The next week when he arrived I jumped into the driver's seat raring to go. Before we even got around the corner he was commenting on my sandals. This time I thought it was very strange, men didn't usually pay this much attention to my shoes. Again, he spent half the lesson watching my feet instead of the road, I began to feel very uncomfortable. After the lesson, he dropped me off and I went in and told my husband about how much time he had spent watching my feet again. He said it was probably just me over reacting but if I didn't feel comfortable with this instructor ditch him and find another one. I had booked three lessons already paid for so I decided to go on the third one and see if I felt any better.

When the next lesson came around and the instructor's car pulled up I was ready for him. Instead of my sandals I had put on a pair of boots, it was still summertime but I felt a bit more comfortable without my toes exposed. As soon as I got into the car the instructor made a comment about my boots. He wanted to know if I wouldn't find it easier to manage the pedals in my sandals. I told him no I was quite alright in my boots. By now I had realised that I had been right about this man, he had a foot fetish. Of all the driving instructors I could have picked out of the phone book I had to find this one. Trust me.

We set off on the lesson. This time he seemed in a bad mood, nothing I did was right, he pulled me up on everything, even though last week he had been delighted with how well I was doing. Halfway through a three point turn he decided the problem was that my boots were in the wrong position on the pedals, they were 'too bulky'. Then he said if I wanted to pull over he had a pair of his wife's flip flops in the boot I could borrow for the rest of the lesson. Alarm bells weren't just ringing by now, they were crashing and banging. I told him I had to get back home and couldn't finish the full lesson, I had just remembered something important. He didn't argue, I think he realised he'd been rumbled. I drove back to my house, jumped out of the car and never saw him again. I don't know how long he kept on being a driving instructor but it definitely wasn't the right job for him, he would have been better off being a chiropodist.

After that I got out the phone book and jumped straight back into finding another instructor. I wasn't going to let one pervert put me off driving, apart from worrying about the foot watcher I had been doing ok. I would just find a better one.

I picked another one and he turned up a week later. This one was a lot younger, not much older than me, I thought I would get on a lot better this time. I should have known better. Five minutes into my first lesson he told me to pull over, I was going to try parallel parking. I told him I had already had a go at that with my last instructor but he said we were going to do it his way. Fair enough, I thought and prepared to move off again. To my surprise, he told me to turn off the engine and then pulled out a big drawing pad and some coloured felt tip pens. He then proceeded to draw three cars, the one we were in plus the two that I would be parking between. This wouldn't have been so bad really if he hadn't taken the time to colour them in, making sure each one was the correct colour for the corresponding car. Oh, my good god, I had gone from a foot fetisher to a nursery school teacher, why did these idiots want to teach people to drive, it was obvious they were in the wrong jobs.

By the time he finished with his drawing another ten minutes had gone from my lesson. Eventually he let me have a go for real, shoving his picture under my nose every ten seconds to better help me understand what I was supposed to be doing. By the time I finally managed to get parked I had made my mind up that I never wanted to see this nutter ever again. First though, we had to get back home. Halfway there, on a busy road we had to pass a cyclist. The fruit cake in the passenger seat told me to give him plenty of room as I passed him, which I did. As I was almost past the cyclist there was a huge bang from the side of the car, I almost died of fright. At first I didn't realise what had happened, I could still see the man on his bike, he was cycling along quite happily. Then there was another loud bang, this time I saw what it was. My nice new friend was kicking the side of the passenger side door. I looked at him in horror,

"What are you doing?" I asked him.

"Do you know what that sound was?" he beamed.

"Yes, you kicking the door." I said.

"Wrong." he yelled. "That was the sound you would have heard if you had hit that man on the bike."

I was completely speechless. He was really pleased with himself, it didn't seem to occur to him that by scaring me half to death I could have just caused a nasty accident. I drove back home as quickly as he would allow me, leaping out of the car as soon as I could get my seat belt off. He called after me,

"Do you want to book another lesson?"

"I'll let you know." I yelled back, running for my front door. I wanted to get inside quickly before he decided to give me his colouring in page to stick up on my fridge.

When my husband came home that night I told him about my latest adventure in driving. He couldn't believe I'd found another nutter, he wanted to know how I always managed to end up with one. I couldn't really help him, I didn't know, I just seemed to have a built-in magnet that attracted them. After all, I told him, that's probably how I'd ended up married to him anyway.

After I had finished filling him in on all the horrific details we came to a decision. Maybe I would be better off finding a nice lady instructor, surely a lady would be a lot calmer and more understanding and wouldn't feel the need to draw pictures, boot the car doors and give me a heart attack for eleven pounds an hour. So, the next day when I had recovered from the shenanigans of the day before, I once again got out the Yellow Pages and began looking for a lady teacher. Let's see how I would fare under a feminine influence. At least it couldn't get any worse. Could it?

You would think by now I would have learned, wouldn't you?

CHAPTER SIXTEEN

Boiled Eggs and Knitting

The day of my first lesson with my new lady instructor came around. She pulled up outside my house and I went outside and got into the car to meet her. She seemed really nice, a plump, homely looking lady in her mid-fifties, she told me her name was Doreen. I filled her in on all the gory details of my two previous instructors and she agreed with me that they both seemed like lunatics. We had a good laugh about it all and set off for our lesson.

It went really well, Doreen was really kind and patient and took time to explain everything properly. She said my driving was good considering what I had been through on all my other lessons (I hadn't told her about the ones with my husband, I was still too traumatised to speak about those). I drove home thinking that finally I had found a good teacher, I would be fine with this one. She dropped me off after the lesson and I booked another lesson for the following week. When my husband came home I told him my troubles were over, I should have picked a woman instructor in the first place. I think he was just glad that he wouldn't have to keep coming home to more horror stories.

I should have known it was too good to be true.

When the next lesson rolled around Doreen pulled up outside and tooted the horn, I ran out and got into the driving seat. We drove out of my street then Doreen told me that for today's lesson we were going for a little tootle in the countryside. That sounded fine to me and I headed off in the direction that Doreen told me to. As we approached the nice quiet country lanes Doreen leant down and took out a plastic bag. Then she said as it was such a lovely day I could just drive around while she finished this bit of knitting. At first I thought she must be joking but no, she was actually pulling some knitting needles and wool from the bag.

"It shouldn't take me long" she said, "I just want to get this sleeve finished, just keep driving and give me a shout if you get stuck."

I couldn't believe it, I had thought Doreen was nice and normal but no, she was just as bonkers as the other two. There was nothing for it but to keep going. I drove along slowly and carefully, praying that nothing would go wrong while she wasn't paying attention to me. Knowing that I was basically on my own was mildly terrifying, Doreen had duel controls on the car but how could she help me out in an emergency if she had her head buried in her knitting?

After I had been driving for a while I turned a bend and saw that a bit further up the road was a crossroads. I didn't know which way I was supposed to go. I asked Doreen if I should turn left or right or go straight on.

"Just a minute." She said, "Let me just get to the end of this row, it's a tricky pattern this one."

She carried on knitting and purling as the crossroads came ever closer, I started to panic.

"Doreen, I don't know which way to go." I pleaded.

"Hang on" she answered. "I don't want to drop a stitch now or the whole bloody thing will be ruined."

"Doreen." I was panicking properly now, I could see quite a lot of traffic up ahead now, all turning in different directions. "Which way?"

Just as I was coming up on the rest of the traffic she finally looked up from her knitting.

"Left" she said. "That's as good a way as any, isn't it?"

With that she went back to her needles leaving me to make the turn and carry on driving. Luckily, before I got into any more trouble she finished the sleeve she was working on and put the knitting back in her bag.

"Goodness me." she said. "Look at the time, that lesson went really quickly didn't it, we'd better head back home now."

I did as I was told and headed off back to my street, thinking the only thing I'd learned today was how to knit two, purl two together and cast off without dropping any stitches. When we got back to my house Doreen asked what time I wanted next week's lesson. I told her I would let her know and made a run for it. Once again, I would be spending the evening scouring the yellow pages.

When my husband came home that night he enquired how my lesson had gone. By the look on his face I could tell that he thought I was making all these things up. It couldn't be possible to just keep finding one nutter after another, nobody else ever went through these things when all they wanted to do was learn to drive. He asked if maybe I thought it was me who was the problem, I seemed to be having an effect on these people. Then he said if I didn't really want to drive I only had to say so, I didn't need to keep coming up with all these mad tales.

I was fuming, how dare he doubt my word. I became even more determined to get my license and without further ado I found myself another instructor before the hour was up, after first making sure she wasn't a knitter.

I had picked another lady teacher. This one was called Caroline and when she turned up I was shocked at how young she was. I was also shocked by how much she smelt of hard boiled eggs. She introduced herself and then after that the first thing she said was,

"This is a brand-new car."

"That's nice." I said.

"I don't want it damaging." she answered.

"I'll try to restrain myself then." I said, trying to lighten the mood.

It quickly became obvious that this woman had zero sense of humour. But I was here now so there was nothing for it but to make the best of it. We ended up driving around the usual routes that I had taken with my other instructors. Every other driving instructor seemed to use the same roads so there were usually quite a few other L plates around. Because they all used the same corners for practicing reversing around, we often had to wait for a vacant one.

I soon found out that Caroline wasn't much for small talk and when she did speak she was very serious about everything. I wasn't really bothered that she didn't speak much as every time she opened her mouth I was assailed by the aroma of boiled eggs. She also drank lots of bottled water while we drove and this caused her to do lots of silent burps so you can imagine how pungent the car was by the end of the lesson.

Nevertheless, I was determined to stick it out with this one, I couldn't face having to go through the rigmarole of finding another teacher, so at the end of the lesson I booked another one for the following week. Apart from the smell of eggs it hadn't gone that badly, at least there had been no knitting or colouring involved and not once had I felt my feet being given unwanted attention. I decided just to try and breathe through my mouth in future.

So followed a few weeks of driving up and down the usual roads in a cloud of boiled egg fumes. Caroline started to open up a bit and even mentioned her boyfriend now and then, although he sounded as boring as she was. I could only assume he had no sense of smell. On the third or fourth lesson, she said she fancied some chocolate and made me drive to a petrol station so she could run in and buy some. Then she made us sit in the nearby car park while she proceeded to eat the lot without offering me so much as a crumb. Greedy cow.

On one lesson, I took a corner a bit too sharpish and clipped the kerb, I thought she was going to have a breakdown. She squealed like a toddler, made me stop the car and then got out and ran around the car shouting.

"Please God, not my wheel rims."

Far too over dramatic in my opinion. I had realised by now that she wasn't a very good teacher, this had become obvious when I was parallel parking one day. She told me the only way to really do it was to turn the wheel, keep an eye on the kerb in my mirror and hope that I ended up in the right position.

"It's all guesswork really." she told me.

I didn't think this was correct but I went along with it anyway just to stop her talking, I couldn't keep on breathing through my mouth all the time, my tongue was starting to dry up. On the way home I quizzed her about her other clients, how many had she got through their driving tests. When she said none, I wasn't too surprised, but she said she had only been in business for a year so that was to be expected. My heart was sinking by now, I realised I was going to have to dump another teacher.

Luckily my cousin Janice saved the day. One of her friends was married to a driving instructor, his name was Dave, she said he was really good and he would take me on as a favour to her. As soon as I had contacted him to book some lessons I rang Caroline and told her that her services were no longer needed. She didn't sound too disappointed, I don't think her heart was really in it and she was far too worried about getting her car damaged. I used to see her when I was on my lessons, driving around with other people and I knew exactly what they were going through. I would try and get a good look at the person driving to see if they were breathing through an open mouth as I had. Since that day, whenever I see a car the same model and colour as hers I instantly get a whiff of boiled eggs, I think I always will.

I knew I had found the right teacher on my first lesson with Dave, we knew a lot of the same people so we had a lot to chat about, although I did get a bit confused when he kept banging on about his new headboard. I wasn't sure why I needed to know about his sleeping arrangements. It took around twenty minutes for me to realise he meant the thing on top of his car with his advert thingy on it. Then, just before the end of my lesson somebody cut me up. Dave rolled down the window and shouted at the driver.

"You daft bastard, can't you see she's a learner?"

He would do for me.

CHAPTER SEVENTEEN

Testing Times

My lessons with Dave were going swimmingly. After the first two or three he decided I was good enough to pass my test and told me to put in the forms and wait for a date. While we waited, I could get in a bit more practice. This sounded fine in theory. All went well until I got a date through for my test, it was to be in three weeks' time. Dave now decided I should have a mock test every lesson now to better prepare me. The first time we attempted this I drove around for a bit and then he told me that when he tapped the dashboard I would be under test conditions. I said ok and waited to hear the tap.

As soon as I heard it I went to pieces, everything I had learnt over the last few weeks disappeared straight from my head. I had no clue what I was doing, I forgot which gear I should be in, which pedal I should be pressing, at one point even which side of the road I should be on. Dave was astonished, he had never seen anyone have such a mental block he said. He told me to pull over, take a deep breath and we would try again.

The second time was even worse, this time I almost screamed when I heard the tap and from then on things went from bad to worse. I wasn't fit to be in charge of a shopping trolley, never mind a car (sorry, killing machine). Dave told me to come out of test conditions immediately. As soon as he said that everything was fine, I went straight back to driving normally, remembering everything I had been taught. It was quite amazing. Dave said that was enough drama for one day, we would practice the test next time when I might not be so nervous. Famous last words.

As the next few weeks went by things got no better. As soon as I heard the tap or heard the words 'test conditions' I would have a complete meltdown and my brain would empty all memories of driving straight out of the window. To make things worse, the actual test was looming, I only had a few days to go. Everyone was offering me advice on how to keep calm, some bright spark even offered me Valium, an offer which I quickly declined. I was in enough of a pickle already, the last thing I needed was to fall asleep at the steering wheel.

At last the dreaded day dawned, I felt terrible, I had been awake half the night, sick with nerves. I kept trying to tell myself it was no big deal, it was twenty-five minutes out of my life and if I failed so what? I would just take the test again. Unfortunately, I wasn't taking any of my own advice and by the time Dave turned up my legs were like jelly. We had a quick last minute lesson on the way to the test centre and Dave gave me his best pep talk although I knew he had serious doubts about me actually getting through the test without passing out.

We got to the test centre and I had to go in and show my driving license. A few minutes later a man called my name and led me off to the car, this was it. I took a last terrified glance at Dave who gave me a thumbs up along with his best encouraging face and then I was in the car park, reading out number plates to this very miserable looking man.

We got into the car, I got my seat belt on, checked my mirrors, started the engine, one final check and we were off. I headed off in the direction the examiner told me to and concentrated hard on trying not to wet myself. I had only been driving for around a minute when I heard it, a grunt coming from the passenger seat. I shot a look at the examiner but he was just looking straight ahead, watching the road. Before another minute had passed I heard it again, this man was definitely grunting, it wasn't a cough, he wasn't clearing his throat, it was a grunt. I didn't know what to think, surely, I can't have ended up in a car with yet another weirdo.

Sure enough, before I got much further up the road he did another one. I soon realised he was doing a grunt roughly once every thirty seconds, we were definitely getting two a minute. My god, as if I didn't have enough to worry about already.

I carried on, turning left, grunt, or right, grunt, whenever I was told. Before long it was time for my parallel parking, it wasn't easy to concentrate with the noises coming from the passenger seat but I managed to get through it without any accidents. Grunter scribbled something on his clipboard and we set off again. Next it was reversing around a corner accompanied once again by frequent grunts. Why the hell hadn't Dave warned me I might get this lunatic, he had told me about several other strange examiners at this centre so I wouldn't get any nasty surprises, how could he forget to mention this one?

To be fair, I was so preoccupied with all this grunting and groaning it actually took my mind off how nervous I was and by the time I got to the end of the test I didn't think I had done too bad. I answered a few questions on the Highway Code and then it was over. I waited with bated breath.

Grunter told me I had failed the test, told me to wait three weeks before taking another test, shoved a piece of paper under my nose and then he was gone, grunting his way across the car park to his next appointment. I wanted to shout after him and tell him nobody would pass a test if they had to share a car with him and all his ridiculous noises, it was very off putting. Before I had time to do anything though, Dave was coming back to the car. As soon as we had switched seats (I wasn't allowed to drive straight after a test) I asked him why on earth he hadn't warned me about the grunter. He said he was sorry, the man used to work there but had left, Dave didn't know that he had come back. He had a look at my fail sheet and said I had only failed on one thing, put straight back in for another test and next time would be a doddle. Even if I got the same examiner I would know what to expect next time. I did as he told me and a few days later I got a date for another test in a months' time.

In the next few weeks while I was waiting I had a few more lessons but Dave said there was nothing he could teach me now, it was just a case of overcoming my nerves on the day.

To make matters worse my husband had already bought me a car of my very own. It was just sitting there, waiting for me to pass my test, he offered to take me out in it but I said no. I was still severely traumatised from our last lessons and had no wish to relive the experience. Every day when I went out to the shops I had to walk past my nice new shiny car, I felt as if it was mocking me.

One afternoon I had to go out to the shops and it was pouring with rain. I looked at my car and thought. The shops were only ten minutes away by car, I knew the roads near my house really well, I had driven them dozens of times now on my lessons. No one would know if I just jumped in the car and went, I could be there and back in half an hour. The fact that I had no license or insurance tried to cross my mind but I shoved that thought to one side.

Feeling really wicked I got in the car and started the engine, now I had got this far there was no turning back. I set off for the shops, driving very slowly and carefully. All went well, I made it to the shops without incident, ran in and got the things I needed then got back in the car and set off for home. I promised myself if I got away with it I would never do this again until I was all legal. Five minutes from home I had to stop at the traffic lights, I was first in the queue. It was only a small narrow road and the lights on the opposite side of the road were quite close. Suddenly I realised I recognised the car opposite me at the other set of lights, it was Dave, taking another lesson and he had seen me. Even though the rain was pouring down I could see him peering between the windscreen wipers to get a proper look.

Oh, god why had I thought I could get away with this. I slithered as far down the driving seat as I could until just my nose was visible above the steering wheel and prayed for the lights to change. When they did I drove straight off, looking in my rear-view mirror I could see Dave twisting round in his seat still watching me. I made it home safely, mentally kicking myself all the way and spent the next few days dreading my next lesson.

The next time Dave pipped his car horn I went outside and jumped in the car. I had decided to play innocent and deny everything. For the first half of the lesson he didn't mention anything and I thought maybe I had got away with it. Then suddenly, out of the blue he said.

"I saw you, you know."

"Saw me when?" I asked, trying to look innocent.

"You bloody well know when." he said.

Then he gave me a lecture about driving without insurance and how I would lose my license before I had even got one if I wasn't careful. I felt about twelve again. I promised I had learned my lesson and that was the end of the matter. Anyway, soon I would be taking my test again and this time I knew I would pass.

I didn't. Despite getting a really nice jolly examiner I blew it again. My examiner was a big elderly man, he looked like a cross between your favourite grandad and Father Christmas and was really encouraging. I was very confident this time. Unfortunately, five minutes away from the test centre when my test was almost over I misjudged another motorist's speed. I was waiting at a junction for my chance to pull out. I should have waited until the other car had passed me but I thought it was far enough away for me to pull out. I heard a sharp intake of breath from my jolly companion as I did so and knew straight away I would be sending off the forms to book another test when I got home.

I was right. The examiner said he had been all set to pass me until I did that. He was very nice about it but said it was too serious a fault to overlook. With a heavy heart, I took my place in the passenger seat and waited for Dave to drive me home again. There would be a few more weeks yet of leaving my car on the driveway as I trudged off shopping on foot. When Dave came back he just said never mind, it would all be ok next time, just be a bit more careful, etc., etc., but I could tell by the look on his face he was wondering how long he was going to be stuck with me.

As it turned out he was stuck with me for another month. When my next test came around I actually passed it. I have no idea how I managed it. I got an awful examiner who seemed to be in a really foul mood. He engaged me in a bit of chit chat but every other word that came out of his mouth was a swear word and he did an awful lot of tutting whenever I attempted a manoeuvre. This time I knew without a shadow of a doubt that I had failed and half way through I made my mind up that I was never going to put myself through this again. I would sell my car and resign myself to being a passenger.

We arrived back in the car park, once again I answered a few Highway Code questions and prepared to hear the news that I had failed once more

You could have knocked me down with a feather when my miserable examiner told me that I had passed. I actually asked him,

"Are you sure"?

"Yes." He replied.

"Well what about the mess I made of my three-point turn?" I asked him.

"Look, you've passed." He said.

"But my emergency stop was a bit crap wasn't it?" I enquired.

He cut me off a bit sharpish there.

"Do you want this bleeding license or not?" He shouted at me.

"Yes please. "I said.

"Well take this, sign this and bugger off."

I thanked him profusely and told him he was going straight to the top of my Christmas card list. He just shook his head and said,

"It's only bloody March."

As he got out of the car though I could see he was smiling. Trying hard not to but still, I saw it.

Dave was over the moon for me, or more probably, for himself. I think he had seen quite enough of me and my driving by this time. He still had to do the driving on the way home though as I couldn't be trusted. I might be too excited and cause an accident. I was more relieved than excited. I had been dreading having to go home and tell everyone I'd failed again.

Back home I rang everyone I could think of to tell them my news. Everyone was pleased and my mother went out and bought me a Congratulations on Passing Your Driving Test card. She even wrote me a little poem inside that she made up. I can still remember it.

At last you've passed your driving test,
We shout hip, hip hooray,
But if I see you coming dear,
I'll still get out the way.

Even now her compliments were still back handed.

CHAPTER EIGHTEEN
Pockets

I was quite enjoying my new freedom now that I had my wheels. It felt a bit daunting at first driving on my own but I soon got the hang of it. The only thing I dreaded was driving my husband anywhere, he still acted as though we were on a lesson and still banged the dashboard every now and then, just to keep me on my toes he said.

At least I never had it as bad as my brother when he got old enough to drive. It also took him a few goes before he passed his test but once he did, as he was still living at home he got the job of ferrying our parents around everywhere. My mother only really wanted taking shopping once a week but my dad took every opportunity to accompany my brother everywhere he went, whether he was invited or not. Now you may remember if you've read my other books that my dad never learned to drive and never owned a car. His one and only experience behind the wheel had occurred when he was eighteen years old and doing his National Service in Singapore. He had moved a lorry from one side of a car park to the other. That was the total extent of his driving experience. However, in his mind this meant that he could drive any time he wanted, no problem, he didn't need a lesson, he already knew how to do it.

He thought this gave him the right to grab the steering wheel from my brother whenever he thought he was getting too close to something. My brother would be happily tootling along up the road when without any warning my dad would wrench the wheel from his grasp whilst shouting:

"BIKE!"

"CAR!"

"KERB!"

Or whatever else he thought my brother was too close to. You will also remember if you have read the other books that my brother, all his life had somewhat of a nervous disposition. Driving with my dad did nothing to cure him of this. He would always return from outings with my dad, white as a sheet and jangling his keys nineteen to the dozen. On one trip into town they ended up completely off the road and in the middle of a busy roundabout. My dad said it was nothing to do with them, that lorry had been too bloody close.

Mind you, whenever I drive anywhere with my mother she too will always warn me when she thinks I'm getting too close to something.

"Mind that bike." She'll say.

"What bike?"

"That one over there." She'll say, pointing to a bike half a mile away on the other side of the road and going in the opposite direction to us. I'll tell her it's nowhere near us but she just tells me it can't hurt to be careful.

"You never know."

"Never know what?"

"You just never know."

My daughter was delighted that I could now drive properly, mainly because she could sit in a seat when we went anywhere now, rather than crouch up on the floor bracing herself for impact. I think she still preferred to go off with her dad in his little work van though. They went all over in it even though it was a mobile tip, full of tools, bags of plaster and weeks' worth of fish and chip papers. In the summer holidays, they always went off camping with my husband's friends and their kids. Their kids were all boys, meaning she was the only girl but that never bothered her. She would spend her days fishing, shooting, swimming, canoeing and doing lots of other things that they never told me about for fear of giving me heart failure. Even now, nearly thirty years later I am still finding out things that would have made my hair fall out, like the time she woke up at four in the morning and sneaked off with the dog to go canoeing on the lake all by herself. I get palpitations just thinking about it. Her dad was so proud of her and would go around telling people she could 'out shoot, out fish and out swim any boy'. She has kept up her love of outdoor activities ever since. I still wonder what the workmen who fitted our windows years later must have thought when they entered her room. She was a teenager by then and her dressing table was full of makeup, jewellery and perfume, sitting in amongst all of the girly things was a massive air pistol that looked like something out of a Dirty Harry movie. I must say they did a good job though and even tidied up after themselves

Her nickname around the time she was seven was 'Pockets' because of all the things she had crammed into them. Every year in September it was a tradition that my dad would buy her a new coat. She would then proceed to ruin said new coat by shoving as much rubbish as was humanly possible into the pockets. She would come trotting out of school with the pockets of her coat halfway around her knees, I despaired of her. And the rubbish she kept in them was nobody's business, she had bits of string, marbles, rocks, batteries, elastic bands, screws, nails, you name it. I would ask her what in the name of god did she need these things for, she would just reply that she might need them one day. Honestly, the contents of her pockets looked like the junk drawer that most people have in their kitchens. I would empty them out and try and sew up all the tears in them but the next day she would come out of the school gates with her pockets dragging around her knees again. I was fighting a losing battle.

My mother also despaired of her and her recent habits, she would follow her around trying to take things off her that were destined for her pockets, then come complaining to me that it wasn't normal (like my mother knew anything about being normal).

"She's been in your dad's bloody shed again." She'd say. "She's got nuts and bolts in her pockets now with all the other stuff." I would tell her it was just a phase and she would grow out of it but my mother was convinced that she was growing up into a kleptomaniac. Once more the blame for all of this fell on my husband's side of the family. No one on our side had ever felt the need to collect bits of junk and carry it around all day. Not for the first time she laid the blame on Frank and Sheila's doorstep. I don't know why because they were as baffled as everyone else by my daughter's pockets.

On one occasion though Pockets saved the day. I had only ever been camping once, when I was at school and I hated every minute of it. Since then I had absolutely no desire to repeat the experience and ran and hid every time someone mentioned the word tent. Every summer I would happily wave Pockets and her dad off on their camping trips and nothing on earth would have persuaded me to go with them. One day though the two of them were nagging me once again to try it, they were trying to tell me that once I got there I would enjoy it. I knew I wouldn't.

In the end, I gave in just to shut them up. I agreed to spend one night in a tent and no more, it was already late afternoon by then so at least I wouldn't have to be there long. Within half an hour the car was packed up and we were on our way. They took me to a campsite by a lake where you could boat and windsurf if you wanted to. We paid at the gate and went in to pitch our tent, the two of them set it up in no time, they'd had plenty of practice. We spent a couple of hours watching the windsurfers and laughing at the ones that kept falling in, then it started to get dark so we went inside the tent and got our sleeping bags out. There was nothing to do but get out the sandwiches we'd brought with us and have our supper. It was September and the nights were starting to get darker earlier, before we knew it we could hardly see a thing. I started looking through our bags for the torch but it wasn't there. In their haste to drag me off before I could change my mind, the two happy campers had forgotten to pack it. Now what were we supposed to do, there were no lights on the campsite except for the shower block and toilets on the other side of the field. By now we could barely see each other.

Then Pockets remembered something she had stashed away in her jacket. For the last few years she had been collecting Sylvanian Families, little families of toy rabbits, mice, squirrels, badgers and other creatures. They all wore clothes and had houses, schools, shops and things. My dad had built my daughter a massive house to keep them all in and it was packed out with little pieces of furniture. One of these pieces was a little lamppost which was kept on the roof garden. For some reason, it had found its way into my daughter's jacket and now she pulled it out from the depths of her pocket. From the other pocket, she produced a little battery and hey presto, we had light. Admittedly not much light but enough to make out each other and our surroundings.

So, there we were, the three of us huddled up in our sleeping bags, eating meat paste sandwiches by the light of a Sylvanian Families lamppost. You couldn't make it up. That was the last time I ever set foot in a tent and I have no intentions of ever setting foot in one ever again unless it's a marquee and it's got proper chairs in it.

At least I learned one thing from my experience, I never nagged my daughter to empty her pockets again. As she kept telling me, you never knew when you might need something in there.

On a last note. I have to say I think Frank and Sheila may have been unfairly judged and it might not have been their dodgy genes in action here regarding my daughter's strange collections. Recently I was clearing out some of my old handbags and as I started to sift through their contents it was like going back in time twenty odd years to the days when I had to empty my daughter's pockets on wash days. Each bag was as cluttered as the one before and I have no idea why I was carrying around some of the junk that I found in there. Just a few examples:

A pair of pliers
Metal tape measure
Three odd batteries
Two light bulbs
Dog biscuits
Five packets of sweeteners
Screwdriver
Scissors
Washing tablets
Giant roll of Sellotape

I think I have to admit that I may know where she got that from.

CHAPTER NINETEEN

What Will the Neighbours Think?

When my daughter was around eight years old my mother decided to go back to work, she wanted something part time, just a few hours a day. To her granddaughter's horror she got a job as a dinner lady at her primary school. That meant that every day, after everyone had eaten lunch, my mother would be in the playground supervising all the children, including all of my daughter's friends.

Now my mother wasn't the most patient woman in the world at the best of times. Sling a couple of hundred kids into the mix and it was only a matter of time before something went wrong. We were all extremely nervous to say the least. I told my daughter to give her a wide berth if possible and try to keep it to herself that they were related.

On my mother's first day I waited until the afternoon when I knew she would be back home then I rang her to find out how it had gone. She said it hadn't been too bad, there were a lot of cheeky little buggers there but she would soon sort them all out. She had already put a few of them in their places. I asked her what she meant by 'putting them in their places', already dreading her reply.

She said she had given a couple of lads a clip round the ear and smacked another one on the back of the legs. Oh, good God. It was only a matter of time before she was clutching some poor unfortunate child round the back of the neck while delivering her trademark slaps to their backside. I told her she wasn't allowed to smack the kids, even the teachers hardly ever smacked them nowadays. She would get herself (and by association, us) into trouble. I already had visions of all the mothers waiting to have it out with me over the things my mother had done. I told her I was too old to be getting beaten up at the school gates.

Over the next few weeks she carried on terrorising the kids in the playground, although I think one of the other dinner ladies had taken her to one side and had a quiet word with her about using actual physical violence. Instead, she just threatened them with it. My daughter told me the other kids used to call her Sergeant Major behind her back. I was hoping either she would get sacked or, failing that my dad might put his foot down and order her to stop working. He was very old fashioned about things like that, he thought if his wife went out to work then the neighbours would think he couldn't afford to support his family. After all these years, he was still worrying about what the neighbours would think.

It was partly because of what the neighbours might think that my parents had never, in thirty years of marriage ever had a proper argument. Instead they had their strange whispered rows in the kitchen with lots of hand gestures and clenched teeth. If they had a disagreement in public they would do the same thing only with fixed polite expressions so that no one else would realise that they were actually having a furious argument.

I had never been able to understand this behaviour. What was the point of having an argument if you couldn't let rip, get everything off your chest and clear the air? Me and my husband (or my husband and I if you want the posh version) always went in for the good old screaming sessions. My mother was appalled at this, she said I hadn't been brought up to scream like a fishwife, obviously rewriting her life again and leaving out the bits where she had screamed blue murder at my brother and me when she was in one of her moods.

What must my neighbours think? She would ask me. I told her everyone argued and it wasn't that big a deal. What about all the times Joan and Colin next door had been having a ding dong and we all sat listening and laughing? She said that was the point, she didn't want people next door pressing their ears to the wall and laughing at her.

Actually, in my house I would sometimes go one step up from shouting and would throw things at my better half. He became very good at ducking over the years, although one night he got his own back. I had cooked pork chops in gravy with vegetables and Yorkshire puddings for his tea and as he was late I put it in the oven to keep warm. He was so late that by the time I served it up it was a shrivelled, dried up mess. Nevertheless, he said it didn't matter, he would eat it anyway so I dished it up, all the time giving him a right bollocking for being so late.

We began bickering and sniping, which started to turn into a full-blown argument. Finally, when I wouldn't let it drop he snapped and threw his plate of dried up pork chops in the air. Unfortunately, he didn't realise how hard he had thrown it, the plate flew across the room like a frisbee, hit the curtains and carried on straight through the window with an almighty crash.

Now it just so happened that the day before this, a new neighbour had moved in next door. And it also just happened that this lady was standing on her doorstep at the time, bidding farewell to some visitors who had come to have a look around her new house. You can imagine her surprise when a plate of pork chops came crashing through the window next to where she was standing and landed at her feet. Unbelievably (or not, if you're familiar with my cooking) the food was so dried up that it didn't move an inch off the plate which had smashed in two.

On the other side of the curtains the pair of us were standing, open mouthed, looking at the giant hole in our window. Unperturbed, my husband went out the front door, nodded his greetings at the poor shocked woman and her equally shocked visitors and said to them:

"I told her I didn't want gravy." before calmly picking up his plate and going back indoors. Talk about first impressions.

When I told my mother about it she was completely horrified. She said there was something wrong with us and that wasn't normal behaviour, I'd obviously picked up these terrible habits from my husband's family. She'd seen Frank and Sheila carrying on like that when they'd been drunk, another thing she didn't approve of. She would say she couldn't understand people who got drunk, she had never been drunk in her life and in thirty years she had never seen my dad drunk. I'd seen him, plenty of times. I asked her what about all the times he came back from the pub acting stupid, like the time he had crept up behind me while I was doing the washing up and shoved my head under the water for a laugh? She said he wasn't drunk, he was just merry. Merry as a newt I thought.

She was always the same, even when my brother got older and started going out drinking. Sometimes he would get so drunk he would get lost on the way home and she would find him laid out in the garden in the early hours. It was never because he had been drinking too much though, it was always the fault of the pub. They had obviously been selling beer that was off and he had been given a bad pint. It was quite amazing how many 'bad pints' he and my dad were served over the years. It's a wonder they never sued the brewery.

My mother stayed at her job as a dinner lady (child tormentor) for another six months, then we all breathed a sigh of relief when she left to take a job as an office cleaner. On her first day there one of the managers jokingly asked her to sit on his knee and take some dictation (that was one brave man). She promptly slapped him round the back of the head and told him she was happily married woman.

She never had much of a sense of humour.

CHAPTER TWENTY

Jolly Holidays

As my daughter got older my parents used to kidnap her for days out, they did enjoy spending time with her but sometimes it was just an excuse for my dad to go somewhere childish where having an actual child with him helped him to blend in. He took her a couple of times to an army museum that he loved where he could spend hours poking around the old stuff. I think she found it quite boring but my dad had a whale of a time climbing on the tanks and pretending to fire the big guns.

When my brother and me were growing up we were always dragged around museums by our parents, they seemed to enjoy them but mainly I think it was because they were free. When I was still an only child I was dragged so often around the transport museum that I probably could have got a job there as the curator. It got so bad that I seemed to develop a museum phobia and have never set foot in one since around the age of twelve. If I think about those days for too long I swear I can still smell the fusty, musty aromas.

Sometimes my dad would take my brother away for the weekend to a bus museum miles away, I think it was in Derbyshire. This was in the days when he was still trying to convince him to be a bus driver, I think maybe that's where his hat came from. After I got married they carried on going on holidays as a threesome, they always stayed in Yorkshire though, never venturing any further north than Whitby. My dad still took endless photos while they were away although by this time my brother had given up pointing at inanimate objects and taken up scowling instead.

Shopping with my dad could be frustrating, whether at home or on holiday because he simply refused to queue for anything. More than two or three people in front of him and he would be off. He said it was bad enough having to part with his hard-earned money, he wasn't bloody queuing for the privilege. When I was at school we learned about Russia and how families once had to stand in queues miles long just for a loaf of bread. I used to think if I had been born in Russia our family would have probably starved to death.

Wherever they went, if it was hot my mother would try her best to stay out of the sun. I think all those years of being covered in oil and vinegar and sizzling away in the garden had put her off it somewhat. She always bought a sunhat and walked on the side of the street that was in the shade. My dad, on the other hand loved the sun, couldn't get enough of it so he would walk on the opposite side of the street to my mother, basking in the sunshine. My brother would spend his time crossing roads, alternating between the two of them. My dad would always come back brown as a berry, my mother would come back as white as when she left and my brother would be somewhere in between the two as he only spent fifty per cent of his time in the sun with one parent and the other fifty per cent in the shade with the other.

After my brother left school and started working my parents were left to holiday alone together. Taking a leaf out of Frank and Sheila's book they decided to venture abroad for the first time ever. Not wanting to leap straight into anything too foreign they started out with Scotland, which was abroad to them even if you didn't need a passport to enter it. They did this for a couple of years on the trot and when that went well they started to venture further afield to places where you actually had to leave Great Britain.

As my mother was too scared to get on a plane at first, they started off with coach trips to Austria and Germany. As I waved them off I felt so sorry for the other passengers who obviously had no idea what they were in for during the next two weeks. I just knew that once they reached Austria my mother would immediately launch into 'Climb Every Mountain' and 'The Hills are Alive with the Sound of Music'. Given half a chance she would be hurtling down a mountainside, arms akimbo a' la Julie Andrews, while my dad hid himself out of sight doing his best impression of the 'Lonely Goatherd'. You can tell how many times I have seen this film.

They arrived home laden down with beer glasses in the shape of boots, women's legs, and god knows what else and straight away my dad was off to the film shop to get his three hundred and sixty-five rolls of film developed. When we saw the photos, it was like looking at the ones from my engagement party again, loads of drunk people standing on long benches, waving huge glasses of beer around and singing German songs. It even looked as though the same 'Oompah' band was there. My mother had a great time she said and had met lots of new friends that she was going to keep in touch with. There were still couples in Scotland desperately trying to get out of being pen pals with my mother and deeply regretting that they had ever agreed to exchange addresses with her in order to send Christmas cards. It would be another twenty-five years before she let them off the hook.

For their next holiday my mother was finally persuaded to get on a plane for the first time in her life. I suggested they try Spain but my mother said that was far too common and would be full of people like Frank and Sheila. Instead they decided to try Greece. Now for someone who didn't care that much for the sun, ten days in Greece in the middle of August didn't seem like the best idea in the world, especially for someone enjoying the hot flushes of menopause but off they went. The minute they stepped off the plane my mother realised she had made a ghastly mistake and wasted no time in buying the biggest sunhat she could find and several handheld fans. Most people would have taken advantage of the hotel's swimming pools to cool down but my parents hated swimming pools, my dad had never learned to swim and went into a blind panic if water went past his ankles and my mother had once perforated her eardrum and lived in fear of getting water in her ears.

I don't think it was their best holiday ever. Apart from the heat they didn't like the food, most of the people, the hotel staff and the transport. One afternoon they went up onto the roof garden of their hotel where you could sit and have a quiet drink. Even now I still don't know quite what went on but somehow, they ended up locked on the roof. Apparently after a certain time of day the roof garden closed, the staff would clear the place of guests and then lock all the doors. Somehow the staff managed to overlook my parents and locked all the doors leaving the pair of them stuck up there.

It was mid-afternoon and boiling hot, I think the heat must have affected them because it's the only reason I can think of to explain what my dad did next. After twenty minutes of banging on all the doors and shouting for help, my dad, who had spent over fifty years trying not to attract any attention to himself picked up a chair and hurled it straight through a large, plate glass window.

I only have their version of events for what followed but my mother said it got very nasty. The staff came running including the manager who threatened to throw my parents out of the hotel if they didn't pay for the damage to the window. My dad refused to pay a penny because it wasn't his fault that someone locked the doors, imprisoning them up there. The manager said there had been three announcements over the hotel's tannoy system, warning the guests that the roof garden was about to close, everyone else had heard it. In the end the holiday rep was called to try and calm the situation down. I don't know how she did it but my parents were allowed to stay for the rest of the week. My mother said that the staff were very 'snotty' with them for the rest of their time there and their breakfasts every morning looked decidedly dodgy. They both said they would never set foot in that country ever again and after that they hated all things Greek. My dad even went off Nana Mouskouri and he had always secretly had a crush on her.

I was completely gobsmacked by these events. In my wildest dreams, I couldn't imagine my dad smashing a window on purpose. I asked my mother what exactly he had been drinking up on the roof because if he hadn't been suffering from heat stroke I could only assume he must have been 'merry'.

Even after they'd been home for a week Greece was still kicking their butts. My mother asked me to set her hair as my cousin Janice was busy that week so I set about putting the rollers in after she'd washed it. Just as I was making a parting for the first roller something ran across her head, making me jump. I cautiously poked at her head again and a whole load more little creatures shot out to join the first one. My mother had caught nits, she must have brought them back from the hotel. When I told her she was mortified, she said her head had been itchy but she had put it down to sunburn, caught on the days she didn't keep her hat on. I had to run out to the chemist to buy some head lice lotion, my mother wouldn't go in case someone saw her and started talking. I told my dad he would need de-nitting as well but he was having none of it. He hadn't caught anything and that was that. I tried to tell him he must have got them as well from sleeping in the same bed as my mother but he was adamant he hadn't got them and refused to discuss it any further. My mother covered her head in the lotion, I was sworn to secrecy and my dad never mentioned it again.

All this drama seemed to have put them off going abroad again and the next couple of holidays they went back to Scotland, they really loved going there and went to the same hotel every time. Just when I thought they would never leave our shores again they decided to have another crack at holidaying in another country. When they told me they had been and booked two weeks away I expected it to be somewhere like Austria or Germany again or maybe a little closer to home, France, or even Jersey. Nothing could have prepared me for the destination they had actually chosen. Las Vegas.

You could not imagine two people less suited to Vegas than my parents, they didn't even like the amusement arcades in Scarborough. They had never gambled in their lives except for the odd game of bingo and Spot the Ball and my dad had no time for the American people who he thought were too loud and showed off a lot (even though he had never met anyone from the US).

Nevertheless, they packed their bags, added a hundred rolls of film for the camera and off they went, my dad had even borrowed a camcorder so that we could see moving pictures as well on their return. It was a ten-hour flight which was another thing that should have put them off seeing as my mother was nervous enough on a short flight but they arrived safely and rang home to let us know they had survived the journey.

We didn't hear from them again for almost two weeks but we assumed no news was good news and if they had caused an international incident we were sure we would have seen it on News at Ten.

They rang home again the night before they left for the airport to remind my brother to get in bread and milk for their return and to make sure he had been walking the dog. He assured them she had been walked every night when he got home from work, this was half true, he did kick her out of the back door into the garden where she walked up and down whilst whining to get back in.

They arrived back clutching an extra suitcase filled with all the tat (souvenirs) that they had bought while they were there. Everything seemed to be dice themed, there were dice clocks, dice mugs, tea towels with dice on them, dice shaped coasters, it went on and on, each piece more tasteless than the one before. They said they'd had a brilliant time, it was a trip of a lifetime. I asked them what they thought of all the casinos but they said they hadn't bothered going in any of them. Then I asked if they had seen any of the big shows but again they said no, they hadn't bothered. I couldn't think how you could go to Vegas and avoid the shows or the casinos but somehow, they had managed it.

I asked what on earth they had been doing for a fortnight then but the photos that my dad had already had developed were coming out of the bag. When I started looking through them it quickly became apparent what they had been doing for the last two weeks - eating.

Practically every photo had a plate of food in it somewhere, there were several of my mother, knife and fork in hand, sitting behind massive piles of chips (fries), sandwiches about a foot tall, huge glasses of ice cream and pies that would feed a family of four for three days straight. On one photo, she looked like Desperate Dan tucking into a cow pie.

They went on and on about the food, how much of it there was, how cheap it was, how many helpings they had managed to shovel down themselves, they had never seen anything like it they said. Admittedly they had another load of photos of themselves sightseeing so at some point they had got up from the table and walked around. As well as raving about the food they had been amazed by the size of the hotels and how many storeys high some of them were. But the highlight of the whole holiday for them had occurred a couple of nights before they left for home. In the hotel lift they had met a couple from the same town as us, not only that but they actually lived a few streets away from my Aunty Dolly, this amazed them more than all the food, lights and hotels put together. They couldn't get over the fact that they had flown half way around the world only to bump into people from a mile up the road. They were simple folk really.

At least there was one good thing, we were spared watching videos of my mother wolfing down half of Vegas as my dad hadn't been able to get the lens cap off the camcorder. It must have been quite a holiday though because all these years later, if anyone mentions Las Vegas, even though sometimes she forgets my name, my mother can immediately recall practically everything she ate during those two weeks she spent in the City of Sin.

CHAPTER-TWENTY ONE

How Very Dare You

A few people who have read my books have commented that most of it must be made up, I can see why they might think that but I assure you everything is true. I have gone through life attracting strange people without even realising I'm doing it. Things are no different today.

My life and that of my family is still just as odd, things still go slightly wonky for us all on almost a daily basis, if there is a mistake to be made out there you can guarantee it will affect us. Appointments still get muddled up, records misplaced and the phrase' Anything that can go wrong will go wrong' should really be our family motto. Our family seem to blunder through life in a series of misunderstandings and crossed wires. From the early days of the mixed-up midwives to the day I took my eleven-year old daughter to the doctors for a sore throat and he asked her how long she had been on the pill. Turned out there was a family with the same name as us living only a few streets away, to have the same last name might not have been too much of a coincidence but most of this family had the same first names as well. For the next few years every time we went to our doctors we discovered more and more of this family's medical history as they probably did about ours.

Then there was the time my husband was chased by the CSA for maintenance for a son he never had, once again it turned out to be the father from the other family although for a short time my daughter was quite excited to have a little brother. The man from the CSA said he was surprised how understanding I had been when presented with the news of my husband's secret offspring. I just told him that after the life I'd had up to now it would take more than that to surprise me.

Then a few years later my husband was quite surprised to find that he'd died unexpectedly. This came about when his sister Anne was shopping in town, she bumped into a girl she knew from years ago who told her she was so sorry to hear the news about her brother. Now Anne thought she was talking about the fact that he'd just broken his leg so she told the girl it wasn't a surprise considering what an idiot he'd always been. The poor girl managed to hide her shock at this remark and asked how I (the grieving widow) was holding up. Anne told her I was getting quite pissed off by now and was sick and tired of running around doing everything by myself. Eventually they realised that they were talking about different things and Anne assured her that her brother was still in the land of the living. We assumed that it must be the other man who lived near us but no, it turned out there was a third person with the same name and it was this poor soul that had died. See? Crossed wires again.

Only about a year ago I found myself in the middle of another major misunderstanding. It started off simply enough, we had changed our car recently and had been left with a tow-bar from the old car that was almost new, it just wouldn't fit the new car. After a few weeks of tripping over this tow-bar I got fed up and so put an advert on the local paper's website to try and sell it.

A few days later I was in B&Q browsing for paint when my mobile rang. I answered it and found myself talking to a man,

"Hello." He said, "I've been looking on the website and I saw your advert on there."

"Oh, right." I replied.

"For the Escort." He said

"Well it's really for a Mazda." I said. This seemed to confuse him so I said,

"If you want to try and make it fit you could always pop round, it might be ok. Its only in the garage."

"Well shall we make an appointment to meet up then?" He said, "I've been looking at your picture and I like what I see."

Now I was the confused one, I didn't know what picture was he talking about, I hadn't put a picture of the tow-bar in the advert.

"What picture?" I asked him.

"Your picture." He said, "On the Escorts website."

The penny finally dropped with an almighty bang. This man didn't want a tow-bar, he wanted a prostitute, I was horrified.

"How dare you. "I screamed down my phone. "I AM NOT A PROSTITUTE!"

This drew a few funny glances from my fellow shoppers but I didn't care, I was mortified. I left without buying any paint and rushed home to tell my husband. I couldn't think what had happened, what the hell category had the paper put my advert in? Was the word 'tow-bar' a euphemism for some kinky thing I didn't know about?

As soon as I arrived home I checked the paper's website for my advert, it was just where it should be, under the motors section along with everyone else trying to sell spare car parts. My husband said it must just be someone who had got the wrong number and laughed it off, after a while I saw the funny side as well. I just wasn't sure I should tell my mother, she would only say it was my fault for wearing dangly earrings and carrying a red handbag.

I forgot about it until a few days later when my phone rang again in the middle of Asda, once again it was some strange man trying to arrange a meeting, or as he put it, 'Book me for the night." This time I just hissed "Wrong number" and hung up, no need to let everyone else at the checkout know my business (not that it was my business). This couldn't be a coincidence, two people pressing the wrong buttons and getting me, somewhere my number was being advertised and not in a good way.

By the end of the week I'd had another two calls and I wasn't finding it funny anymore, my husband was less amused by now as well. The next day, once more my phone rang and sure enough it was another strange man asking about a 'date'. I passed the phone to my husband who let this man know, in no uncertain terms that he was barking up the wrong tree.

This man got all flustered and hung up but he had left his number, I rang him back straight away and asked him where he had seen my number, he said he would tell me if I would promise to delete his number as he was terrified of his wife finding out. He gave me details for a website and hung up quickly, I could hear the terror in his voice and I thought maybe I had done his wife a favour, he might be too nervous to try this again with a real escort.

We checked the website but couldn't find anyone with my number, I decided it was easier to change my number than spend hours trolling through adverts for 'Honey B' and 'Juicy Lucy' so that's what I did. A few days later my new career as an escort was over, though it did cross my mind that I could have made a few bob there. Not as an escort you understand, but by blackmailing all these dodgy blokes who didn't want their wives to find out what they were up to.

By the way, we never did sell the tow-bar, I continued to trip over the bloody thing for another few weeks before slinging it onto the back of the rag and bone man's cart when he did his rounds.

We just seem to be a family that attracts confusion on a regular basis. Even our dog was sent to see a psychiatrist, they called it 'Canine Behaviourist' but I knew what it meant. Our bulldog was a very nervous girl (hardly surprising, living in our family) but lately she had been getting a lot worse. The vet suggested this doggy shrink woman and, as the insurance paid for it I agreed. Really, I just wanted to see what a dog psychiatrist really did for £100 an hour, would she make my dog lie on a little couch and talk about when she was a puppy?

It turned out all she did was avoid all eye contact with my dog while throwing dog biscuits at her. Meanwhile she quizzed me about all her problems. The worst problem she had was going for other dogs, she was so scared that they would attack her that she would try and get in first. She's a big, heavy, strong dog and I would usually end up sitting on her until the other dog had passed which drew lots of sniggers from passers-by. The woman told me there was a simple solution to this one. She told me to take a bag of chicken (my dog's favourite food) whenever we went walkies. Then if she saw another dog I was to throw the chicken on the ground so that she would concentrate on that and ignore the other dog. I had already tried this one before, all that happened was my dog wolfed the chicken down at lightning speed and then attacked the other dog for looking at her food. She got the best of both worlds, dinner and a fight.

In the end the visit was a complete waste of time and petrol, this woman was about as much use as a chocolate teapot and made not one iota of difference to my dog. It opened my eyes though to how easy it was to make a lot of easy money from a lot of gullible people.

So you see, going through life things just seem to happen to me and mine all the time. I'm sure other people have the same experiences, just with longer breaks in between.

CHAPTER TWENTY-TWO

Twist and Go

The broken leg mentioned in the last chapter was just the latest in a long line of injuries suffered by my husband, usually as a result of him doing something stupid. His earliest major scar comes from the time when he was about seven or eight. In those days, just about everyone's grandad had saved bits of shrapnel or bullets from the war and they were all over the place. He had found a bullet and decided to hit it with a hammer to make it shoot the garden fence, something he had seen John Steed do on The Avengers on TV.

The resulting blast blew most of the palm of his hand off and took Sheila's kitchen window out at the same time. I think that was his first operation. The latest one (the broken leg) had occurred when he was fiddling with his latest motorbike. He kicked it off in the garage and it kicked back with such force that it blew him up into the air where he hit his head on the ceiling and knocked himself out. When he came to, he realised the bottom half of his leg didn't seem to have any bones in it and his foot was on backwards. Still in shock he grabbed hold of his foot and twisted it back round to its correct position. Luckily, he twisted the right way and avoided a corkscrewed leg. Then he shouted me to get the car and get him to hospital.

Straight away I realised this must be serious, he would never go to near a doctor unless it was something bad. Usually he fixed his own injuries with the help of his trusty medical kit, this consists of a tube of superglue and a roll of Sellotape. To be fair, I have seen him perform some minor miracles in the past using his kit.

Anyway, I loaded him into the back of the car and headed off for the hospital. After parking up I went and got a wheelchair and pushed him into A&E. We were met by a nurse who asked what the problem was. I explained what had happened and described the injury. She peered at his foot and said not to worry, it might just be a sprain.

"His foot was on backwards." I told her.

"Well that doesn't necessarily mean anything's broken." She said.

"But his foot was on backwards." I repeated. "His toes were facing behind him."

"Let's not jump to conclusions." She insisted. "A twisted ankle can be very painful you know." This woman was obviously a simpleton.

"Look I understand about twisted ankles." I told her. "I've had a twisted ankle myself before but it never twisted 180 degrees."

Still she persisted.

"Let's wait and see what the X Ray shows, you might be surprised."

If it wasn't broken I would be more than surprised, I would be absolutely gobsmacked. She wheeled him off for an X Ray while I stayed outside and waited. After a few minutes a doctor came rushing by me and went into the X Ray room closely followed by another one. A few minutes later Nurse Dopey came out looking a bit flustered.

"Is it broken then?" I asked her.

"Just a bit." She whispered, and then scurried off to be totally unhelpful to the next person.

To cut a long story short most of the bottom bit of his leg ended up somewhere around his kneecap and after a week in hospital (where there was another mix up and they forgot to feed him anything but a small pot of jam for two days) he was sent home with mostly metal where his bones used to be.

I'd hoped that would be the end of the injuries and he would have learned to be more careful but since then he's managed to break a couple of ribs, dislocate his elbow and somehow shift his good kneecap a few inches further away from where it should be. I have now given up on him completely, some people just cannot be helped.

Sometimes I feel as if I had two children and the big one needs keeping an eye on far more than the little one ever did. He goes through life taking no notice whatsoever of his surroundings, lurching from one mishap to the next. His eyesight is appalling but trying to drag him to the opticians is like trying to drag a dog to the vets, combine his awful eyesight with his dyslexia and it's asking for trouble.

A couple of years ago he was having trouble sleeping so the doctor gave him some tablets. He took one the first night but it didn't help, he was up and down all night going to the toilet. The next day he was exhausted so at bedtime he took two pills. This night went even worse, the next morning he was in a terrible mood.

"Those stupid tablets don't work at all" he said "I've been up and down again peeing all night, I took another one at three o clock this morning but I still didn't sleep. I didn't drink that much last night, how could I be peeing so much?"

I said I didn't know but then I got a horrible feeling I might know after all. I had been given some water tablets (diuretics) ages ago but I hardly ever took any, the box was still in the cupboard and looked a lot like the box of tablets that he had been given. With a sinking feeling I went to look in the cupboard, sure enough there was the box he had been given unopened, next to the box of water tablets with several missing. No wonder the idiot had been up all night peeing for England.

Of course, he said it was my fault for leaving them near to each other, even if he wasn't dyslexic the writing on the box was that small that he wouldn't have been able to read it anyway. The rest of us had a good laugh for a few weeks after that one.

This wasn't his first mistake by any means, in the past he's had many including in the middle of the night drinking from what he thought was a carton of milk only to find it was fabric softener. There was the time he was brushing his teeth with hair conditioner and telling me he didn't think much to that toothpaste in the gold tube, (it tasted foul and it didn't foam), and spraying his armpits with air freshener to name but a few. Only last month he had another 'mistake', this one was a corker and had all the younger members of the family in stitches for ages.

He had been complaining that his eyes were sore so I bought some eye wash and told him I had left it in the cupboard for him before I went out. When I came home he was complaining that his eyes were burning.

"That eye spray you bought me is rubbish" he said "It's made them ten times worse."

"What spray?" I asked, "I bought you eye wash not spray, what have you used?"

It turned out he had picked up the spray that's meant to numb your throat when it's sore, it's a wonder he didn't blind himself. I couldn't believe he'd done it again. He said that would explain why at first, he hadn't realised anything was wrong, his eyes were numb.

It's got to the stage now where I am thinking of putting child locks on all of the cupboards to keep him away from anything harmful. I thought I had enough to do looking after my mother but he's worse, he told me once he was terrified of getting dementia when he's older. I told him if he did it would probably take a couple of years before I realised anything was different.

CHAPTER TWENTY-THREE

End of the Line

Reading back through these chapters I can hardly believe it was all so long ago, it only feels like a few years.

Since those days, the years have flown by, Christmases seem to come around twice as fast and birthdays even faster. Before I even get used to being one age, another birthday smacks me in the face and I have to try and remember my new age. Not that it really matters as I have been thirty-nine for quite a few years now, it can be quite embarrassing as my daughter is now only five years younger than me.

My mother cannot understand why I lie about my age, she says she is proud of every one of her years and has been known to actually add a couple of years on to her real age. I have never been able to understand women who tell the truth about their age, especially the elderly ones who accost you in the street to tell you how old they are. At what age does this happen? Do you just wake up one day and suddenly feel the need to go up to complete strangers and blurt out "I'm eighty-five you know?" I hope not, I'm planning to be thirty-nine for the next twenty years at least. If I really have to I may increase it to forty-two but no more than that.

These old ladies seem to treat their advancing years as some sort of badge of honour. My mother had a neighbour who, on her eightieth birthday began telling everyone,

"I'm nearly eighty-one you know", even though her next birthday was three hundred and sixty-four days away. She would repeat this every birthday until the day she died at the age of eighty-nine although on her gravestone I'm sure it will have said 'Nearly ninety."

My little great nieces and nephews have no idea of my real age, it's a closely guarded secret. They're always bugging their mums to find out, not that they're any the wiser either and they run a little sweepstake between them, each one trying to guess the correct age. When Christmas and Birthdays are coming up their guesses seem to be quite a lot younger, bless em. They are also banned from calling me 'Great Aunty' too, no matter how much they try to convince me it's because I'm so 'great'.

My daughter grew up and carried on the family tradition of chaos and confusion. She married a man who is a carbon copy of her father, he goes through life lurching from one misunderstanding to the next and is even more accident prone than his Father in Law. He has far more scars and operations under his belt and at the time of writing still falls off ladders while clutching chainsaws, electrocutes himself and runs up trees on sit on lawnmowers on a regular basis.

Sometimes we look back and we realise that he really wasn't this bad at the start. My husband seems to have influenced him quite a lot. Whenever they are together we both get quite nervous, it's like the blind leading the blind. A few years ago, my husband decided to get into boating and bought a knackered old cabin cruiser. He took his Son- In-Law off with him on his maiden voyage and before half an hour had passed they were stuck out at sea waiting for the coastguard to rescue them. When the coastguard arrived, my husband recognised them as the same team that had been sent out to rescue him and his friends the year before when his jet ski hit a sandbank and got wedged. On that occasion, half the rescue team got stuck as well, my husband ended up pulling them from the mud and sand and they all ended up getting rescued together.

As you can imagine, they were very pleased and delighted to be meeting up with him yet again. Some of them had tears in their eyes.

My daughter's wedding day was as eventful as mine was too. At the last minute. the zip on her wedding dress got stuck and as she climbed into her wedding limo my husband was right behind her with a pair of pliers trying to unstick it and zip her up. One of her little bridesmaids chose that very moment to pull at a thread on her bridesmaid's dress, thus unravelling the stitching that was holding the whole bottom ruched part up. That meant I was chasing the bridesmaids into the car with a needle and cotton trying to stitch her back up again. History repeated itself again when both me and the groom's mother turned up in the same shoes, holding the same bags. Luckily, they were getting married in a large hotel so they didn't have the same experience as I did when the guests had to avoid the cowpats in the churchyard. Having said that she had the same 'magical' wedding night as I had when everyone got far too drunk, she and her new husband had a massive fight and spent the night planning to get divorced as soon as possible.

Luckily, also like me, they soon got over it and have now been happily (mostly) married for fifteen years. She's still surrounded by animals and birds so nothing much has changed there and a couple of years ago she was found by a passer-by hanging upside down by one welly from a tree that she had climbed trying to rescue her falcon who had become entangled in a branch. As you can imagine she is quite well known in her village, well people point a lot anyway.

My mother is still going strong although we lost my dad a few years ago. He died as he lived, trying not to make a fuss and I still miss him every day. Wherever he is I imagine him sitting with my Aunty Dolly who went a few years before him, she is giving him grief for letting my mother get so lazy and leaving me to do everything and he is hiding his eyes, mortified at the things my mother wears now that he's not there to keep her in line.

My mother now lives in a little flat in sheltered accommodation with a lot of other elderly people. It reminds me a lot of a primary school, they all gang up on each other, friends change on a daily basis and someone is always running to the manager of the place to tell tales to 'Miss'.

She spends her days watching telly, eating, playing bingo, doing 'keep fit' without actually getting out of the chair and gossiping with all the other old ladies. I have listened in sometimes but it gets very repetitive. None of them have much of a memory so every day they spend hours telling each other the same thing they told each other the day before. She struggles with technology so I have to write little notes of instruction for everything, the TV remote, the telephone, the toasty maker, it's all beyond her.

A few months ago, she rang me at eight o clock in the evening.

"Did you just ring me?" She asked. I said no, I hadn't.

"Well someone did, I was on the loo and I didn't get there on time."

I told her to check her Caller ID button but she didn't know what I meant. I told her to read the instructions I had left her and she went off to check. A few minutes later she rang back.

"It's the police, what do the police want with me, what have I done?" She was frantic.

"How do you know it's the police?" I asked

"Because it says CID" she said, she hadn't worked out that CID stood for Caller ID.

There's no wonder I worry.

I tell her time and time again not to open her door to anyone without looking through the peephole and asking to see identification. She says if she could reach up high enough to see through the peephole she would, but she says she's not daft, she wouldn't let anyone in unless she knew them.

"You can't be too careful" she said to me a few weeks ago, "I was only saying that the other day to that man that was here."

"What man?" I asked her.

"Oh, just some man who came round selling tea towels and stuff."

"And you let him in?"

"Well yes but only because he said he'd been in the other flats as well."

"Did it not cross your mind that he might have been lying?"

"No, he didn't look like a liar, he looked honest."

"Oh well that's Ok then isn't it? Are you mad, he could have been a serial killer."

"Well I don't know about that but his dishcloths are rubbish, they're falling apart already."

Sometimes I despair of her, she lives in her own little world, you wouldn't think she watched the news every day.

As she has got older she has also developed a terrible wind problem. To put it nicely, she could fart for England. Any little movement results in a giant fart and once she's out of her chair and hobbling towards the kitchen each step is punctuated by a fart. Because she is so deaf now she can't hear the farts even though she obviously knows she's doing them. This gives her the impression that nobody else can hear them either so she completely ignores them and carries on with whatever she's doing, leaving everyone around her trying not to laugh out loud. I feel sorry for the other residents that have to get into the lift with her every day. Still she's happy in her own little world just as long as I keep showing up with her food every day.

Recently she was sent by her doctor to see a dietician. Even now there are still a few of them determined to make her lose weight, the rest of us have completely given up on this. As usual I had to go along. When the lady started quizzing my mother on her daily eating habits I couldn't believe my ears. She tried to convince the poor woman that she had no appetite whatsoever and found it hard to eat anything. By the end of the discussion this woman was under the impression that my mother lived on two slices of bread and a cup of tea every day.

She was somewhat puzzled by how someone who ate so little could be so large so I gently reminded my mother of the cream cakes, meat pies, biscuits, sweets, ice cream and chips that accompanied these two slices of bread on the average day. She then told the woman that it was all my fault and that she only ate them because I brought them for her. I then got a telling off from the dietician who told me I should try and encourage her more.

I took no notice, I know from years of experience that my life wouldn't be worth living if I turned up with a bag of healthy food. In desperation, the dietician tried to frighten my mother by telling her she would soon develop diabetes. This didn't faze my mother one iota, she just told her that wouldn't matter because she knew where you could buy special chocolate for diabetics.

Most days when I pass my dad's photo at home I ask him what the hell he was thinking, leaving me to deal with this madwoman on my own. He just smiles back, obviously enjoying the peace and quiet.

And so, we come to the end of my family saga. Looking back, I'm really glad I was born when I was, I think the Seventies were definitely the best time to be a teenager. I would hate to be one of today's teenagers, it all looks far too much like hard work. We thought we knew it all but we were a lot more innocent than they are today (Oh my god I sound old).

I'm sure in the future there will be many more mix ups, crossed wires, general confusion and embarrassing situations in our lives. Maybe one day I'll fill a few more pages of life as an elderly confused teenager, my daughter will have to help me fill in the blanks though because no doubt my brain will be too addled by then. Then again, she probably won't be too far behind me in the memory stakes. She seems to spend most of her days fighting against the same things that that I do, things that drive a person nuts and sometimes she gets so wound up she has trouble remembering her own name. She tells me she looks around at her life and wonders why she was never born into a normal family.

I definitely know where she gets that from!

The End

21541121R00131

Printed in Great Britain
by Amazon